IELTS
Testbuilder

Sam McCarter and Judith Ash

MACMILLAN

Macmillan Education
Between Towns Road, Oxford OX4 3PP
A division of Macmillan Publishers Limited
Companies and representatives throughout the world

ISBN 978 1 405 01403 8 (Book)
ISBN 978 1 405 01404 5 (Pack)

Page layout by eMC Design
Illustrated by Paul Collicut

The authors would like to thank Roger Townsend, Dr R A Young
and the students who kindly supplied the authentic student
writing answers.

The publishers would like to thank Louis Harrison,
Susan Hutchison, Anne Kilraine and Lynne Pollard.

The author and publishers would like to thank the following for
permission to reproduce their material:
Dr Sue Beckerleg for the adapted article 'Learning methods'; Pam
Brabants for the adapted article 'Eva Hesse'; Carl Chandra for the
adapted articles 'Networking' and 'Day-dreaming – an art or a waste
of time?'; Reproduction of extract 'Worms put new life into derelict
site' © Mimi Chakraborty/Times Newspapers Limited, London, 22
September 1996; Caroline Hammond for the adapted article 'Adam's
wine'; Peter Hopes for the adapted article 'Variations on a theme: the
sonnet form in English poetry'; Phil Jakes for the adapted articles
'Great escapes' and 'Waterside: a study in suburban development';
Ruth Midgley for the adapted article 'Musical instruments
reclassified'; Micky Silver for the adapted article 'A profession
undervalued'; Roger Townsend for the adapted article 'A silent force';
The University of Cambridge Local Examinations syndicate for the
IELTS sample answer sheets and scoring bands.

The authors and publishers would like to thank the following for
permission to reproduce their photographs:
Stone/Getty; p118
The Estate of Eva Hesse/Galerie Hauser & Wirth; p59

Audio CDs produced by James Richardson at Studio AVP. Musical
extract from 'Invention in Eb' by Micky Silver (2000).

Printed in Thailand

2014 2013 2012
17   16   15

CONTENTS

INTRODUCTION   4

IELTS TESTBUILDER

The IELTS Testbuilder is more than a book of Practice Tests. It is designed not only to enable you to practise doing tests of exactly the kind you will encounter in the exam itself, but also to provide you with valuable further practice, guidance and explanation. This will enable you to prepare thoroughly for the exam and increase your ability to perform well in it. The IELTS Testbuilder has been developed for students who are aiming to achieve a minimum of Grade 6 in the academic component of the IELTS exam.

IELTS Testbuilder contains:

Four complete Practice Tests for the academic version of the International English Language Testing System

These tests closely reflect the level and types of question to be found in the exam.

Further Practice and Guidance pages

In each test, these follow each paper or section of a paper.

For the READING AND LISTENING TESTS, the Further Practice and Guidance pages contain exercises, questions, advice and tips directly related to each paper or section. They encourage you to reach your own decisions as to what the answers in the tests should be. Their step-by-step approach enables you to develop and apply the appropriate processes when answering the questions in the exam.

For the WRITING TEST, they contain language development exercises, help with planning and a range of authentic sample answers for you to assess.

For the SPEAKING TEST, there are examples of possible question areas, guidance in topic development and suggestions for useful language.

Key and Explanation

This contains full explanations of answers in the Tests and Further Practice pages. For multiple-choice and Yes/No/Not Given questions, there are clear and detailed explanations not only of the correct answer, but also of why the other options are incorrect.

How to use the IELTS Testbuilder

1 Simply follow the instructions page by page. Clear directions are given as to the order in which to do things. If you follow this order, you:

- complete one part of a paper, perhaps under exam conditions, and then

either

- do the Further Practice and Guidance pages relating to that part. You then check the answers to the questions in those pages and review the answers given to the questions in the test in the light of what has been learnt from doing the Further Practice and Guidance pages. After that, you can check the answers to the questions in the test and go through the explanations.

Or

- check the answers to the questions in the test and go through the explanations if there are no Further Practice and Guidance pages and

then

- move on to the next part of the test.

Note that in some cases it is necessary to do the Further Practice section before completing the relevant section of the paper.

2 Vary the order.

You may wish to do some of the Further Practice and Guidance pages before answering the questions in the test that they relate to.

Alternatively, teachers may wish to do the Further Practice and Guidance pages as discussion or pairwork, or ask students to prepare them before class.

The International English Language Testing System

The following is a brief summary of what the exam consists of. Additional details of what is tested in each Paper are given in the relevant Further Practice and Guidance pages.

THE LISTENING MODULE   approximately 30 minutes

Contents	Situations	Question Type
There are four separate sections which you hear only once. There are usually 40 questions. You have time to read the questions and time at the end to transfer your answers to the answer sheet. As the test progresses, the difficulty of the questions, tasks and text increases.	The first two sections are of a general, social nature. There will be a conversation between two people and then usually a monologue or an interview. In the third and fourth sections, the contexts are of an educational or training nature. There will be a conversation of up to four speakers and then a talk/lecture of general academic interest.	The question types may include: • multiple-choice questions • sentence completion • short answer questions • completion of tables/charts/summaries/notes • labelling a diagram • matching.

THE ACADEMIC READING MODULE   60 minutes

Contents	Texts	Question Type
There are three reading passages with a total of 1,500 to 2,500 words. There are usually 40 questions. You must write your answers on the answer sheet within the 60 minutes. As the test progresses, the difficulty of the questions, tasks and text increases.	The texts are of the type you find in magazines, journals, textbooks and newspapers. The topics are not specific to any one discipline. They are all accessible to candidates who are entering undergraduate or postgraduate courses. There is at least one article which contains detailed logical argument.	The question types may include: • multiple-choice questions • sentence completion • short answer questions • completion of tables/charts/summaries/notes • choosing headings • identification of a writer's views or attitudes (Yes/No/Not Given) • classification • matching lists • matching phrases.

THE ACADEMIC WRITING MODULE   60 minutes

Contents	Task Type	Assessment Criteria
Task 1 You are advised to spend 20 minutes and write a minimum of 150 words.	You will be asked to write a report about a graph, table, bar chart or diagram.	You will be assessed on your ability to: • answer the question which is asked • use English grammar and vocabulary • use language that is appropriate in style, register and content • write in a way that your reader can follow.
Task 2 You are advised to spend 40 minutes and write a minimum of 250 words.	You will be asked to express your opinion of a point of view, problem etc. or to discuss a problem.	You will be judged on your ability to: • write in an appropriate style • present a solution to the problem • justify your opinion • compare and contrast your evidence and opinions • evaluate and challenge ideas.

THE SPEAKING MODULE   11–14 minutes

Contents	Task Type	Assessment Criteria
There are three sections: Part 1 (4–5 minutes) Introduction and interview	The examiner will introduce himself/herself, check your identification and then ask you questions about yourself, your home, interests etc.	In all parts of the speaking module, you will be assessed on your: • fluency and coherence • vocabulary • grammatical range and accuracy • pronunciation.
Part 2 (3–4 minutes) Individual long turn	You will be given a card with a subject on which you will be asked to prepare a short talk of 1–2 minutes. You will be given a pencil and paper to make notes.	
Part 3 (4–5 minutes) Two-way discussion	You will take part in a discussion with the examiner on a subject related to the one in Part 2.	

For notes on how IELTS is scored, see page 175.
For further information about the exam see also the IELTS Handbook and www.IELTS.org.

TEST ONE

LISTENING approximately 30 minutes

Before listening to the recording and completing Sections 1–4, go on to pages 14–15.

SECTION 1   QUESTIONS 1–10

Questions 1–5

Complete the details below.

*Write **NO MORE THAN TWO WORDS** or **A NUMBER** for each answer.*

Example
Identification and security check: Platinum *Card* Service

Card number: 6992 **1**................. 1147 8921

Name: Carlos da Silva

Postcode: **2**.....................

Address: **3**..................... Vauxhall Close, London

Date of birth: 13 July **4**...................

Mother's maiden name: **5**.....................

Questions 6–10

Circle the correct letters A–C.

6   The caller has paid

    A   less than the computer shows.

    B   more than the computer shows.

    C   £500 twice.

7   The caller is also worried about

    A   a bill that is too high.

    B   an overpayment to a restaurant.

    C   a payment that he does not recognize.

8   The interest

    A   went up in April.

    B   has not changed.

    C   has gone down.

9   The caller's number is

    A   020 7997 9909.

    B   020 7989 7182.

    C   020 8979 7182.

10   The operator will ring the caller

    A   tomorrow.

    B   in two hours.

    C   very soon.

Stop the recording when you hear 'That's the end of Section 1'.
Now check your answers to Section 1 of the test.

SECTION 2   QUESTIONS 11–20

Questions 11–13

*Circle the correct letters **A–D**.*

11   Mr Gold had problems because he

    A   hated smoking.

    B   smoked.

    C   couldn't touch his toes.

    D   was very lazy.

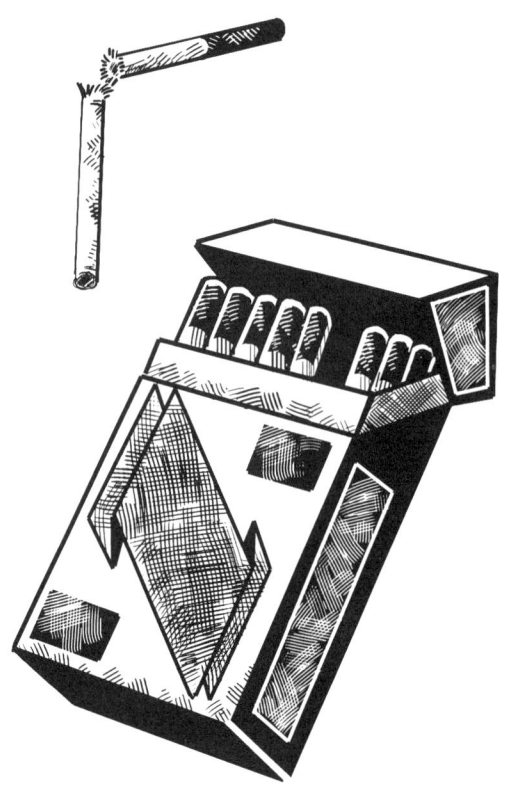

12   Mr Gold used to travel across London to

    A   get exercise.

    B   see London at night.

    C   get cigarettes.

    D   buy food.

13   What did Mr Gold have difficulty with in the past?

    A   running

    B   giving up smoking

    C   getting to sleep at night

    D   getting up early in the morning

Questions 14–20

*Write **NO MORE THAN THREE WORDS** for each answer.*

14   Mr Gold stopped smoking on ....

15   Mr Gold said he was .... if people had not seen him smoking.

16   The worst side effects he experienced were ....

17   He saw giving up smoking as an ....

18   It was easier for Mr Gold to stop smoking than he had ....

19   The radio presenter would like to have Mr Gold's ....

20   The presenter hopes listeners will find their own .... to success.

Stop the recording when you hear 'That's the end of Section 2'.
Now check your answers to Section 2 of the test.

SECTION 3   QUESTIONS 21–30

Questions 21–23

Write NO MORE THAN TWO WORDS for each answer.

Lorraine

- has been with them on the course for **21**............................ .

- has left because she has got a **22**............................ .

- has returned to **23**............................ .

Questions 24–30

Circle the correct letters A–D.

24   Steve's mark could have been better if he had

    A   not made mistakes in his project.

    B   done a better book review.

    C   written more words.

    D   chosen a different topic for his project.

25   Steve's book review was

    A   too long.

    B   not as good as his project.

    C   excellent.

    D   fairly good.

26   Steve's tutor criticizes which aspect of his project?

    A   the beginning

    B   the argument about road pricing

    C   the end

    D   the length

27   The tutor recommends that Frances should do

    A   a PhD but not an MPhil.

    B   an MPhil or a PhD.

    C   another project.

    D   her work more carefully.

28   As regards getting funding, the tutor thinks Frances's

    A   chances are slim.

    B   chances are greater than many other students'.

    C   exam results will be decisive.

    D   chances are better now than in the past.

29   The last time a student in the department achieved a first in their exams was

    A   three years ago.

    B   thirty years ago.

    C   last year.

    D   in the first three years the college was open.

30   Steve does not plan to go on to do research because he wants to

    A   stop studying.

    B   do lots of really exciting things.

    C   earn some money to do the things he would like to do.

    D   ˙return to his job.

Stop the recording when you hear 'That's the end of Section 3'.
Now check your answers to Section 3 of the test.

SECTION 4   QUESTIONS 31–40

Questions 31–33

Write **NO MORE THAN THREE WORDS** *for each answer.*

Notes:

The speaker specializes in management **31**............................ .

Bullying in the workplace costs the **32**............................ up to
£4 billion a year.

Bullying is caused by
* insufficient experience,
* insecurity, or
* a lack of **33**............................ on the part of managers.

Questions 34–40

Write **NO MORE THAN THREE WORDS** for each answer.

Main methods of bullying

- Setting **34**........................... tasks.

- Constantly moving the goalposts.

- Stopping individuals **35**........................... to criticism.

- Not **36**........................... or replying to e-mails. This means you cannot

  expect your staff to **37**........................... you.

- Using technology. Companies should develop an **38**........................... of

  practice.

Task

In groups **39**........................... other bullying strategies

and ways in which they can be **40**........................... .

Stop the recording when you hear 'That's the end of Section 4'.
Now check your answers to Section 4 of the test.

FURTHER PRACTICE FOR LISTENING SECTIONS 1–4

PREDICTION SKILLS

Preparation for listening is an important aspect of this part of the examination. Looking carefully at the questions can help you to predict a number of things, both about what you are going to hear and the answer that is required. The following exercises will give you practice in predicting answers.

GAP-FILLING 1

It is important that you develop the skill of predicting the content of each gap to be filled.

Look at Section 1 on page 8 and for questions 1–5 make notes about what type of information is needed.

1   ....

2   ....

3   ....

4   ....

5   ....

MULTIPLE-CHOICE QUESTIONS

With multiple-choice questions, it can be useful to change the stem into a question. This prepares you to listen for the answer you need.

For example, questions for the answers required for questions 1–5 are as follows:

1   What are the missing numbers in the credit card number?

2   What is the postcode?

3   What is the house number?

4   What is the caller's date of birth?

5   What is the maiden name of the caller's mother?

Now make questions for 6–10 on page 9.

6   ....

7   ....

8   ....

9   ....

10   ....

KEY WORDS

It can also be helpful to listen out for key words. These could be in the question, in the stem of the multiple-choice question, or in the gap-fill sentence. When you hear these words you know that the answer is near.

However, remember that the words or phrases themselves may not be heard on the recording; they may be paraphrased. In addition, the answer may come before the key word or phrase that you are listening for.

Look at Section 2, questions 14–20 and underline the key words or expressions to listen for.

GAP-FILLING 2

Some questions ask you to fill gaps in sentences, notes or summaries. For these tasks, it is important to think about the grammar of the answer that is needed.

Look at Section 4, questions 31–40 and make notes about the grammar of the answer that is needed in each case.

31 ....

32 ....

33 ....

34 ....

35 ....

36 ....

37 ....

38 ....

39 ....

40 ....

Now check your answers to these exercises. When you have done so, listen to the recording and complete the tasks in Sections 1–4 on pages 8–13.

ACADEMIC READING 60 minutes

READING PASSAGE 1

*You should spend about 20 minutes on **Questions 1–15** which are based on Reading Passage 1 below.*

NETWORKING

Networking as a concept has acquired what is in all truth an unjustified air of modernity. It is considered in the corporate world as an essential tool for the modern businessperson, as they trot round the globe drumming up business for themselves or a corporation. The concept is worn like a badge of distinction, and not just in the business world.

People can be divided basically into those who keep knowledge and their personal contacts to themselves, and those who are prepared to share what they know and indeed their friends with others. A person who is insecure, for example someone who finds it difficult to share information with others and who is unable to bring people, including friends, together does not make a good networker. The classic networker is someone who is strong enough within themselves to connect different people including close friends with each other. For example, a businessman or an academic may meet someone who is likely to be a valuable contact in the future, but at the moment that person may benefit from meeting another associate or friend. It takes quite a secure person to bring these people together and allow a relationship to develop independently of himself. From the non-networker's point of view such a development may be intolerable, especially if it is happening outside their control. The unfortunate thing here is that the initiator of the contact, if he did but know it, would be the one to benefit most. And why? Because all things being equal, people move within circles and that person has the potential of being sucked into ever growing spheres of new contacts. It is said that, if you know

eight people, you are in touch with everyone in the world. It does not take much common sense to realize the potential for any kind of venture as one is able to draw on the experience of more and more people.

Unfortunately, making new contacts, business or otherwise, while it brings success, does cause problems. It enlarges the individual's world. This is in truth not altogether a bad thing, but it puts more pressure on the networker through his having to maintain an ever larger circle of people. The most convenient way out is, perhaps, to cull old contacts, but this would be anathema to our networker as it would defeat the whole purpose of networking. Another problem is the reaction of friends and associates. Spreading oneself thinly gives one less time for others who were perhaps closer to one in the past. In the workplace, this can cause tension with jealous colleagues, and even with superiors who might be tempted to rein in a more successful inferior. Jealousy and envy can prove to be very detrimental if one is faced with a very insecure manager, as this person may seek to stifle someone's career or even block it completely. The answer here is to let one's superiors share in the glory; to throw them a few crumbs of comfort. It is called leadership from the bottom.

In the present business climate, companies and enterprises need to co-operate with each other in order to expand. As globalization grows apace, companies need to be able to span not just countries but continents. Whilst people may rail against this development it is for the moment here to stay. Without co-operation and contacts, specialist companies will not survive for long. Computer components, for example, need to be compatible with the various machines on the market and to achieve this, firms need to work in conjunction with others. No business or institution can afford to be an island in today's environment. In the not very distant past, it was possible for companies to go it alone, but it is now more difficult to do so.

The same applies in the academic world, where ideas have been jealously guarded. The opening-up of universities and colleges to the outside world in recent years has been of enormous benefit to industry and educational institutions. The stereotypical academic is one who moves in a rarefied atmosphere living a life of sometimes splendid isolation, a prisoner of their own genius. This sort of person does not fit easily into the mould of the modern networker. Yet even this insular world is changing. The ivory towers are being left ever more frequently as educational experts forge links with other bodies; sometimes to stunning effect as in Silicon Valley in America and around Cambridge in England, which now has one of the most concentrated clusters of high tech companies in Europe.

It is the networkers, the wheeler-dealers, the movers and shakers, call them what you will, that carry the world along. The world of the Neanderthals was shaken between 35,000 and 40,000 BC; they were superseded by *Homo sapiens* with the very 'networking' skills that separate us from other animals: understanding, thought abstraction and culture, which are inextricably linked to planning survival and productivity in humans. It is said the meek will inherit the earth. But will they?

Questions 1–5

Do the following statements agree with the information in Reading Passage 1?

In boxes 1–5 on your answer sheet write

YES	*if the statement agrees with the information*
NO	*if the statement contradicts the information*
NOT GIVEN	*if there is no information about the statement*

Example	*Answer*
Networking is a concept.	Yes

1   Networking is not a modern idea.

2   Networking is worn like a badge exclusively in the business world.

3   People fall into two basic categories.

4   A person who shares knowledge and friends makes a better networker than one who does not.

5   The classic networker is physically strong and generally in good health.

Questions 6–10

*Using **NO MORE THAN THREE WORDS** from the passage, complete the sentences below.*

6 Making new acquaintances ...., but also has its disadvantages.

7 At work, problems can be caused if the manager is ....

8 A manager can suppress, or even totally ...., the career of an employee.

9 In business today, working together is necessary in order for .... to grow.

10 Businesses that specialize will not last for long without ....

Questions 11–15

*Using **NO MORE THAN THREE WORDS** from the passage, answer the questions below.*

11 In which sphere of life have ideas been protected jealously?   ....

12 Which type of individual does not easily become a modern networker?   ....

13 Where is one of the greatest concentrations of high tech companies in Europe?   ....

14 Who replaced the Neanderthals?   ....

15 What, as well as understanding and thought abstraction, sets us apart from other animals?   ....

Before you check your answers to Reading Passage 1, go on to pages 19–20.

FURTHER PRACTICE FOR READING PASSAGE 1

The questions below will help you to make sure that you have chosen the correct answers for questions 1–5 on Reading Passage 1.

Question 1 *Look at the first sentence of paragraph one and answer the following questions.*

1   Which adjective qualifies the phrase 'air of modernity'?

....

2   What is the meaning of the word 'unjustified'?

   a   not valid

   b   not real

   c   without justice

   d   without truth

3   What does the word 'acquired' mean?

....

4   Does the sentence below agree with the text?

   The writer states that networking is an old concept.

....

Question 2 *Look at the last sentence of paragraph one and answer the following questions.*

1   What does the word 'concept' refer to?

....

2   Does the text restrict the wearing of the badge to the business world? Or is it talking generally?

....

3   Which phrase in the last sentence tells you this?

....

Question 3 Look at the first sentence of paragraph two and answer the following questions.

1   How many types does the writer say people can be divided into?

     ....

2   Does the text mention a number?

     ....

3   Therefore, do you know how many types of people there are? Is the information given?

     ....

Question 4 Look at the first three sentences of the second paragraph and answer the following questions.

1   Who shares things with others?

     ....

2   Who doesn't share?

     ....

3   Does the text make a direct comparison between the two types?

     ....

4   Is it clear from the text which type of person is better at networking?

     ....

Question 5 Look at the second paragraph and answer the following questions.

1   What does the word 'strong' mean in the text?

     ....

2   Does the text mention physical weakness or not being physically strong?

     ....

3   Does the text mention anything about general health?

     ....

Now check your answers to these exercises. When you have done so, decide whether you wish to change any of your answers to Reading Passage 1. Then check your answers to Reading Passage 1.

READING PASSAGE 2

*You should spend about 20 minutes on **Questions 16–27** which are based on Reading Passage 2 below.*

A SILENT FORCE

A   There is a legend that St Augustine in the fourth century AD was the first individual to be seen reading silently rather than aloud, or semi-aloud, as had been the practice hitherto. Reading has come a long way since Augustine's day. There was a time when it was a menial job of scribes and priests, not the mark of civilization it became in Europe during the Renaissance when it was seen as one of the attributes of the civilized individual.

B   Modern nations are now seriously affected by their levels of literacy. While the Western world has seen a noticeable decline in these areas, other less developed countries have advanced and, in some cases, overtaken the West. India, for example, now has a large pool of educated workers. So European countries can no longer rest on their laurels as they have done for far too long; otherwise, they are in danger of falling even further behind economically.

C   It is difficult in the modern world to do anything other than a basic job without being able to read. Reading as a skill is the key to an educated workforce, which in turn is the bedrock of economic advancement, particularly in the present technological age. Studies have shown that by increasing the literacy and numeracy skills of primary school children in the UK, the benefit to the economy generally is in billions of pounds. The skill of reading is now no more just an intellectual or leisure activity, but rather a fully-fledged economic force.

D   Part of the problem with reading is that it is a skill which is not appreciated in most developed societies. This is an attitude that has condemned large swathes of the population in most Western nations to illiteracy. It might surprise people in countries outside the West to learn that in the United Kingdom, and indeed in some other European countries, the literacy rate has fallen to below that of so-called less developed countries.

E   There are also forces conspiring against reading in our modern society. It is not seen as cool among a younger generation more at home with computer screens or a Walkman. The solitude of reading is not very appealing. Students at school, college or university who read a lot are called bookworms. The term indicates the contempt in which reading and learning are held in certain circles or subcultures. It is a criticism, like all such attacks, driven by the insecurity of those who are not literate or are semi-literate. Criticism is also a means, like all bullying, of keeping peers in place so that they do not step out of line. Peer pressure among young people is so powerful that it often kills any attempts to change attitudes to habits like reading.

F   But the negative connotations apart, is modern Western society standing Canute-like against an uncontrollable spiral of decline? I think not.

G   How should people be encouraged to read more? It can easily be done by increasing basic reading skills at an early age and encouraging young people to borrow books from schools. Some schools have classroom libraries as well as school libraries. It is no good waiting until pupils are in their secondary school to encourage an interest in books; it needs to be pushed at an early age. Reading comics, magazines and low brow publications like Mills and Boon is frowned upon. But surely what people, whether they be adults or children, read is of little import. What is significant is the fact that they are reading. Someone who reads a comic today may have the courage to pick up a more substantial tome later on.

H   But perhaps the best idea would be to stop the negative attitudes to reading from forming in the first place. Taking children to local libraries brings them into contact with an environment where they can become relaxed among books. If primary school children were also taken in groups into bookshops, this might also entice them to want their own books. A local bookshop, like some local libraries, could perhaps arrange book readings for children which, being away from the classroom, would make the reading activity more of an adventure. On a more general note, most countries have writers of national importance. By increasing the standing of national writers in the eyes of the public, through local and national writing competitions, people would be drawn more to the printed word. Catch them young and, perhaps, they just might then all become bookworms.

Questions 16–22

Reading Passage 2 has eight paragraphs labelled **A–H**.

Choose the most suitable heading for each paragraph from the list of headings below.

Write the appropriate numbers (i–xii) in boxes 16–22 on your answer sheet.

One of the headings has been done for you as an example. Any heading may be used more than once.

Note: There are more headings than paragraphs, so you will not use all of them.

List of Headings

i	Reading not taken for granted
ii	Taking children to libraries
iii	Reading: the mark of civilization
iv	Reading in St Augustine's day
v	A large pool of educated workers in India
vi	Literacy rates in developed countries have declined because of people's attitude
vii	Persuading people to read
viii	Literacy influences the economies of countries in today's world
ix	Reading benefits the economy by billions of pounds
x	The attitude to reading amongst the young
xi	Reading becomes an economic force
xii	The writer's attitude to the decline in reading

---

16   Paragraph **A**

17   Paragraph **B**

18   Paragraph **C**

19   Paragraph **D**

20   Paragraph **E**

21   Paragraph **F**

22   Paragraph **G**

Example	Paragraph **H**	*Answer* **vii**

Questions 23–27

Do the following statements agree with the information in Reading Passage 2?

In boxes 23–27 on your answer sheet write

YES	*if the statement agrees with the information*
NO	*if the statement contradicts the information*
NOT GIVEN	*if there is no information about the statement*

Example
  According to legend, St Augustine was the first person to be seen reading silently.
Answer
  Yes

---

23   European countries have been satisfied with past achievements for too long and have allowed other countries to overtake them in certain areas.

24   Reading is an economic force.

25   The literacy rate in less developed nations is considerably higher than in all European countries.

26   If you encourage children to read when they are young the negative attitude to reading that grows in some subcultures will be eliminated.

27   People should be discouraged from reading comics and magazines.

Before you check your answers to Reading Passage 2, go on to pages 25–26.

FURTHER PRACTICE FOR READING PASSAGE 2

The questions below will help you to make sure that you have chosen the correct options for questions 16–22 on Reading Passage 2.

Question 16 *Look at paragraph A and answer these questions.*

1   Does the paragraph describe the development of reading from one point of time to another?

     ....

2   Is the paragraph only about reading as it was in St Augustine's day?

     ....

3   Is the theme of the paragraph how reading became a mark of civilization?

     ....

Question 17 *Look at paragraph B and answer these questions.*

1   Does the paragraph talk about modern nations?

     ....

2   Are educated workers in India mentioned as an example of something in the paragraph?

     ....

3   Is the first sentence of the paragraph the topic sentence, and the rest of the paragraph exemplification?

     ....

Question 18 *Look at paragraph C and answer these questions.*

1   Is the importance of reading in an economic sense the theme of the paragraph?

     ....

2   Does the paragraph show how reading as a skill is now an economic force?

     ....

3   Is the amount of money that reading has contributed to the economy the central idea of the paragraph?

     ....

Question 19 Look at paragraph D and answer these questions.

1   Is a problem described in this paragraph?

    ....

2   Does the paragraph only mention the fact that reading is taken for granted in developed societies?

    ....

3   Are both a reason and a result discussed in this paragraph?

    ....

Question 20 Look at paragraph E and answer these questions.

1   Does the paragraph say that young people today are attracted to reading?

    ....

2   Does this paragraph describe the various ways young people regard reading?

    ....

3   Is the writer's attitude to reading discussed?

    ....

Question 21 Look at paragraph F and answer these questions.

1   Is the question about the attitude of modern Western society to the decline in reading?

    ....

2   According to the text, can this decline be controlled?

    ....

3   Does the writer answer a question by giving his or her own opinion?

    ....

Question 22 Look at paragraph G and answer these questions.

1   Does the paragraph describe how to encourage reading?

    ....

2   Does the paragraph talk about young people and their attitude to reading?

    ....

3   Do the instructions for the exercise specify that each of the headings can be used only once?

    ....

Now check your answers to these exercises. When you have done so, decide whether you wish to change any of your answers to Reading Passage 2. Then check your answers to Reading Passage 2.

READING PASSAGE 3

*You should spend about 20 minutes on **Questions 28–40** which are based on Reading Passage 3 below.*

Variations on a theme: the sonnet form in English poetry

A   The form of lyric poetry known as 'the sonnet', or 'little song', was introduced into the English poetic corpus by Sir Thomas Wyatt the Elder and his contemporary Henry Howard, Earl of Surrey, during the first half of the sixteenth century. It originated, however, in Italy three centuries earlier, with the earliest examples known being those of Giacomo de Lentino, 'The Notary' in the Sicilian court of the Emperor Frederick II, dating from the third decade of the thirteenth century. The Sicilian sonneteers are relatively obscure, but the form was taken up by the two most famous poets of the Italian Renaissance, Dante and Petrarch, and indeed the latter is regarded as the master of the form.

B   The Petrarchan sonnet form, the first to be introduced into English poetry, is a complex poetic structure. It comprises fourteen lines written in a rhyming metrical pattern of iambic pentameter, that is to say each line is ten syllables long, divided into five 'feet' or pairs of syllables (hence 'pentameter'), with a stress pattern where the first syllable of each foot is unstressed and the second stressed (an iambic foot). This can be seen if we look at the first line of one of Wordsworth's sonnets, 'After-Thought':
  'I thought of thee my partner and my guide'.
If we break down this line into its constituent syllabic parts, we can see the five feet and the stress pattern (in this example each stressed syllable is underlined), thus:
'I <u>thought</u>/ of <u>thee</u>/ my <u>part</u>/ner <u>and</u>/ my <u>guide</u>'.

C   The rhyme scheme for the Petrarchan sonnet is equally as rigid. The poem is generally divided into two parts, the octave (eight lines) and the sestet (six lines), which is demonstrated through rhyme rather than an actual space between each section. The octave is usually rhymed **abbaabba** with the first, fourth, fifth and eighth lines rhyming with each other, and the second, third, sixth and seventh also rhyming. The sestet is more varied: it can follow the patterns **cdecde**, **cdccdc**, or **cdedce**. Perhaps the best interpretation of this division in the Petrarchan sonnet is by Charles Gayley, who wrote: "The octave bears the burden; a doubt, a problem, a reflection, a query, an historical statement, a cry of indignation or desire, a vision of the ideal. The sestet eases the load, resolves the problem or doubt, answers the query or doubt, solaces the yearning, realizes the vision." Thus, we can see that the rhyme scheme demonstrates a twofold division in the poem, providing a structure for the development of themes and ideas.

D   Early on, however, English poets began to vary and experiment with this structure. The first major development was made by Henry Howard, Earl of Surrey, altogether an indifferent poet, but was taken up and perfected by William Shakespeare, and is named after him. The Shakespearean sonnet also has fourteen lines in iambic pentameter, but rather than the division into octave and sestet, the poem is divided into four parts: three quatrains and a final rhyming couplet. Each quatrain has its own internal rhyme scheme, thus a typical Shakespearean sonnet would rhyme **abab cdcd efef gg**. Such a structure naturally allows greater flexibility for the author and it would be hard, if not impossible, to enumerate the different ways in which it has been employed, by Shakespeare and others. For example, an idea might be introduced in the first quatrain, complicated in the second, further complicated in the third, and resolved in the final couplet – indeed, the couplet is almost always used as a resolution to the poem, though often in a surprising way.

E   These, then, are the two standard forms of the sonnet in English poetry, but it should be recognized that poets rarely follow rules precisely and a number of other sonnet types have been developed, playing with the structural elements. Edmund Spenser, for example, more famous for his verse epic 'The Faerie Queene', invented a variation on the Shakespearean form by interlocking the rhyme schemes between the quatrains, thus: **abab bcbc cdcd ee**, while in the twentieth century Rupert Brooke reversed his sonnet, beginning with the couplet. John Milton, the seventeenth-century poet, was unsatisfied with the fourteen-line format and wrote a number of 'Caudate' sonnets, or sonnets with the regular fourteen lines (on the Petrarchan model) with a 'coda' or 'tail' of a further six lines. A similar notion informs George Meredith's sonnet sequence 'Modern Love', where most sonnets in the cycle have sixteen lines.

F   Perhaps the most radical of innovators, however, has been Gerard Manley Hopkins, who developed what he called the 'Curtal' sonnet. This form varies the length of the poem, reducing it in effect to eleven and a half lines, the rhyme scheme and the number of feet per line. Modulating the Petrarchan form, instead of two quatrains in the octave, he has two tercets rhyming **abc abc**, and in place of the sestet he has four and a half lines, with a rhyme scheme **dcbdc**. As if this is not enough, the tercets are no longer in iambic pentameter, but have six stresses instead of five, as does the final quatrain, with the exception of the last line, which has three. Many critics, however, are sceptical as to whether such a major variation can indeed be classified as a sonnet, but as verse forms and structures become freer, and poets less satisfied with convention, it is likely that even more experimental forms will out.

Questions 28–32

Reading Passage 3 has six paragraphs labelled **A–F**.

Choose the most suitable heading for each paragraph from the list of headings below.

*Write the appropriate numbers (**i–xiii**) in boxes 28–32 on your answer sheet.*

One of the headings has been done for you.

Note: There are more headings than paragraphs, so you will not use all of them.

List of Headings

i   Octave develops sestet

ii   The Faerie Queene and Modern Love

iii   The origins of the sonnet

iv   The Shakespearean sonnet form

v   The structure of the Petrarchan sonnet form

vi   A real sonnet?

vii   Rhyme scheme provides structure developing themes and ideas

viii Dissatisfaction with format

ix   The Sicilian sonneteers

x   Howard v. Shakespeare

xi   Wordsworth's sonnet form

xii   Future breaks with convention

xiii The sonnet form: variations and additions

Example	Paragraph **A**	*Answer* **iii**

28   Paragraph **B**

29   Paragraph **C**

30   Paragraph **D**

31   Paragraph **E**

32   Paragraph **F**

Questions 33–37

*Using **NO MORE THAN THREE WORDS** from the passage, complete the sentences below.*

33   Sir Thomas Wyatt the Elder and Henry Howard were ....

34   It was in the third decade of the thirteenth century that the ....
was introduced.

35   Among poets of the Italian Renaissance .... was considered to be
the better sonneteer.

36   The Petrarchan sonnet form consists of ....

37   In comparison with the octave, the rhyming scheme of the sestet is ....
varied.

Questions 38–40

*Choose the correct letters **A–D** and write them in boxes 38–40 on your answer sheet.*

38   According to Charles Gayley,

    A   the octave is longer than the sestet.

    B   the octave develops themes and ideas.

    C   the sestet provides answers and solutions.

    D   the sestet demonstrates a twofold division.

39   The Shakespearean sonnet is

    A   an indifferent development.

    B   more developed than the Petrarchan sonnet.

    C   more flexible than the Petrarchan sonnet.

    D   enumerated in different ways.

40   According to the passage, whose sonnet types are similar?

    A   Spenser and Brooke

    B   Brooke and Milton

    C   Hopkins and Spenser

    D   Milton and Meredith

Now check your answers to Reading Passage 3.

ACADEMIC WRITING   60 minutes

TASK 1

You should spend about 20 minutes on this task.

> *The graph below compares the number of visits to two new music sites on the web.*
>
> *Write a report for a university lecturer describing the information shown below.*

Write at least 150 words.

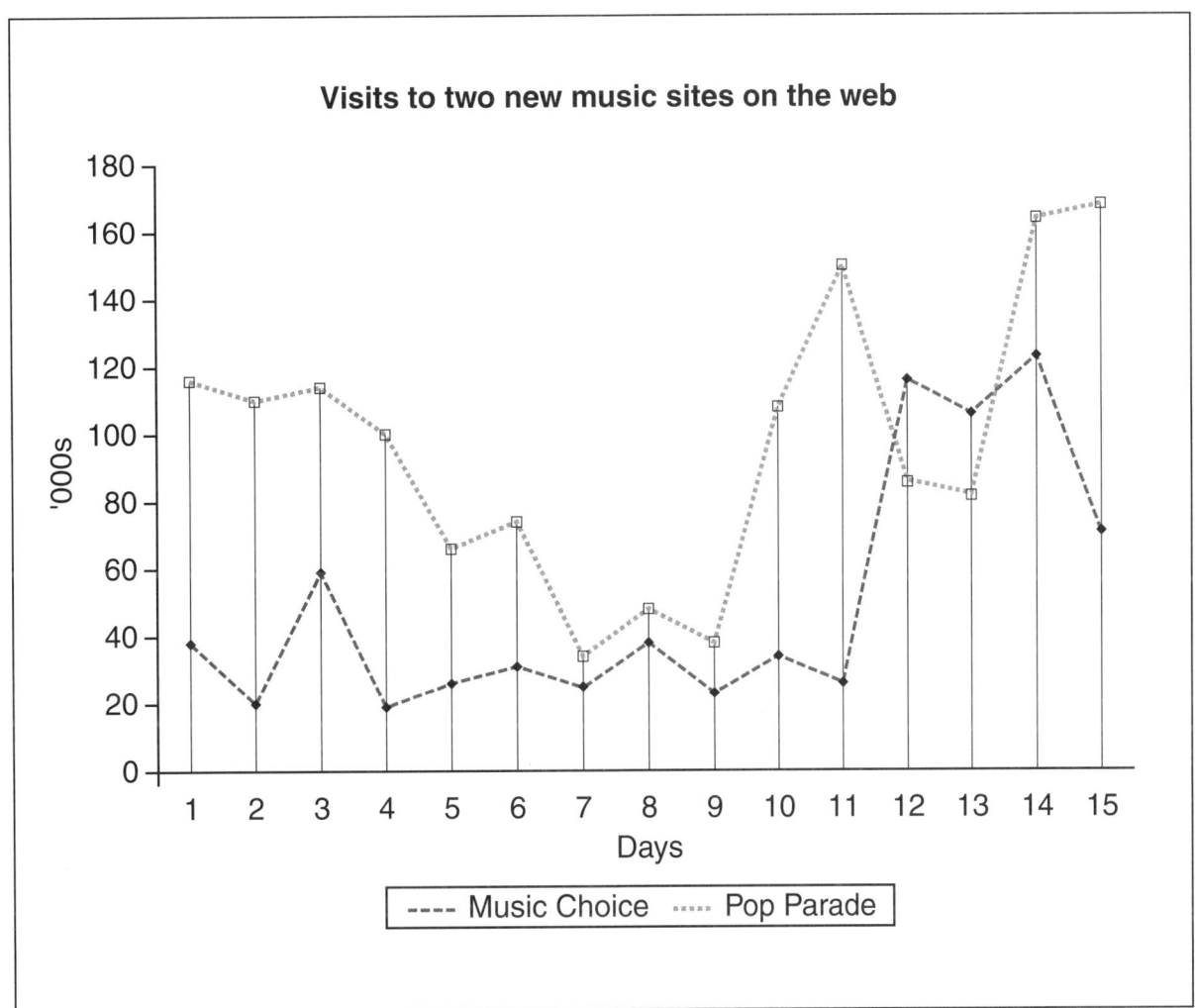

Before you write your answer to Task 1, go on to pages 32–34.

FURTHER PRACTICE FOR TASK 1

LANGUAGE DESCRIBING MOVEMENTS IN GRAPHS

1   *Match the statements **a–l** with the graphs **1–8** below. For example, statement **a** matches graph **8**. Some graphs can be used more than once.*

   a   Sales rocketed over the period.

   b   The purchase of furniture was rather erratic, hitting a peak in the middle of the period.

   c   The sale of fish products rose dramatically.

   d   There was a slight dip in equipment production.

   e   There was a steady increase in the amount of coal used, followed by a period of stability.

   f   There were wild fluctuations in sales, but the trend was upward.

   g   The number of people attending the weekly lectures plunged.

   h   There was rather a dramatic fall in the share price.

   i   Share prices plummeted, but then stabilized.

   j   After a dramatic fall in the number of people settling in the city, there was a period of stability.

   k   The number of houses sold dipped slightly.

   l   There was a gradual decline in the number of children visiting the zoo.

Graphs

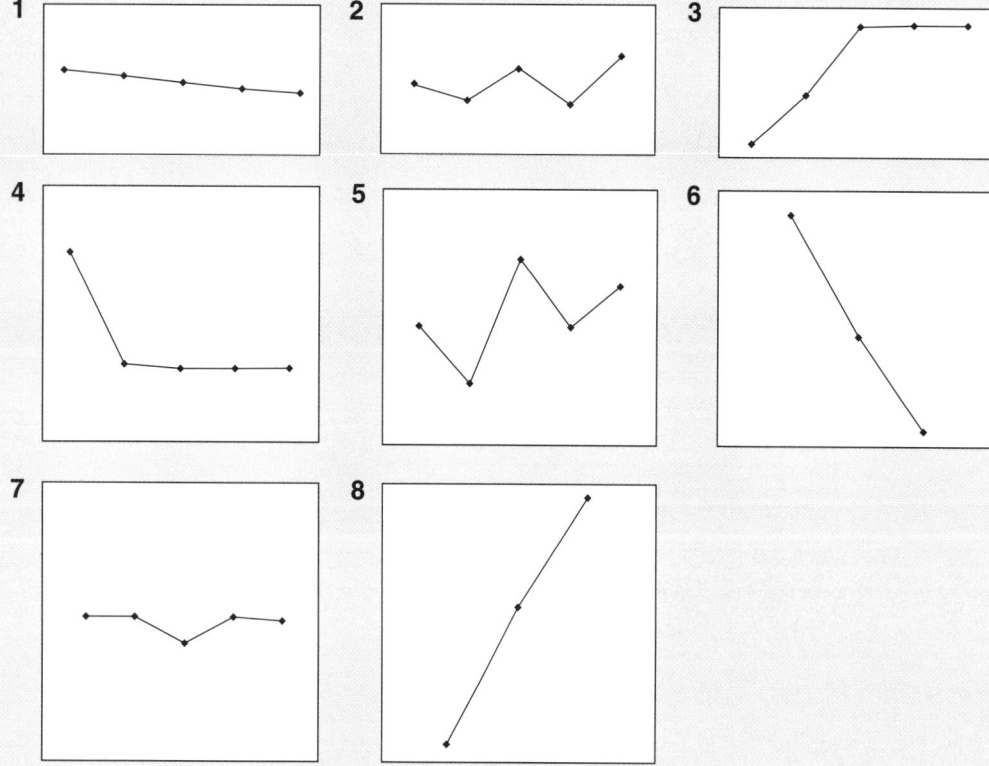

2   *Look at the graph in Task 1 on page 31 and read the following sentences, which relate only to the Music Choice site. Try to complete the sentences.*

a   The number of *hits to Music Choice .... to 60,000 on Day 3.

b   On the fourth day, the number of visitors to the Music Choice site ....
by 66%, to 20,000.

c   There was .... in hits to the Music Choice site on the third day.

d   On the fourth day, there was .... in the number of visitors to
the site.

e   On Day 13, the number of hits .... slightly.

f   On the second day, the number of hits .... to 20,000.

g   The number of hits .... within a narrow margin from Day 4 to
Day 11.

h   On Day 13, the number of site visitors .... slightly, before
hitting a new peak of just over 120,000 on Day 14.

i   The number of hits .... significantly on Day 15.

j   The number of visitors to the Music Choice site reached .... of
just over 120,000 on Day 14.

   * or *visits to*

*Look at the items in the box below. Which can be used instead of the phrases you wrote in **a–j** above? There may be more than one answer and you may use each item more than once.*

halved	a gradual rise	fluctuated	plunged	a new peak
dipped	a steep fall	soared	a sharp rise	rocketed	fell back

Now check your answers to these exercises. When you have done so, go on to page 34.

3   *Now write your own answer to Task 1 on page 31. When you have finished writing your report, use questions **a–g** below to help you check what you have written.*

   a   Is the length of the text appropriate?

     ....

   b   Does the text answer the question?

     ....

   c   Are there any common mistakes in the text? If so, what are they?

     ....

   d   Is there any repetition of words or phrases?

     ....

   e   Is anything missing?

     ....

   f   Are the paragraphs well linked together? If so, in what way?

     ....

   g   Does the report contain a wide range of vocabulary and structures?

     ....

4   *Now look at the following model answer to Task 1 and answer questions **a–g** above.*

The graph shows the number of hits to two new music sites on the web, measured in thousands over a period of fifteen days. As far as Music Choice is concerned, the number of visits to the site fluctuated between 20,000 and 40,000 in the first eleven days, except for Day 3 when they reached 60,000. By contrast, visits to the Pop Parade site fell erratically from approximately 120,000 hits on Day 1 to around 40,000 on Day 7.

Between days 11 and 15 visits to Music Choice fluctuated dramatically, hitting a peak of over 120,000 on Day 14. Despite a drop to less than 40,000 hits, Pop Parade saw a huge increase in the number of hits between Days 9 and 11, reaching a total of over 150,000 hits on Day 11. At the end of the fifteen-day period the number of hits to Pop Parade peaked at around 170,00, whereas those for Music Choice showed a marked decline to around 70,000.

(164 words)

Now check your answers to this exercise and compare your report with the authentic student answer on page 134. Then do Task 2 on page 35.

TASK 2

You should spend about 40 minutes on this task.

Write about the following topic:

Some people believe that computers are more a hindrance than a help in today's world. Others feel that they are such indispensable tools that they would not be able to live or work without them.

- *In what ways are computers a hindrance?*
- *What is your opinion?*

Give reasons for your answer and include any relevant examples from your own knowledge or experience.

Write at least 250 words.

When you have written your answer to Task 2, compare it with the authentic student answer on page 134.

SPEAKING   11–14 minutes

PART 1   INTRODUCTION AND INTERVIEW (4–5 MINUTES)

In this part of the examination you will first be asked your name and then you will be asked questions about yourself. Answer these possible questions:

1   How long have you been studying?

2   What subjects have you found the most difficult to study?

3   What do you enjoy/dislike about studying?

4   Have you gained/Do you hope to gain any qualifications?

5   Do you hope to do any further studies in the future?

Now look at the Further Practice section on page 37.

PART 2   INDIVIDUAL LONG TURN (3–4 MINUTES)

You will have to talk about the topic on the card for one to two minutes. You have one minute to think about what you are going to say and make some notes to help you if you wish.

Describe your journey to school or work.

You should say:

- what forms of transport are involved
- the importance of time
- whether it is enjoyable or not

and explain how you would make your journey more pleasant if you could.

Now look at the Further Practice section on page 37.

PART 3   TWO-WAY DISCUSSION (4–5 MINUTES)

In this part of the exam, the examiner will discuss a topic with you. The topic is usually related in some way to the topic in Part 2, but the questions will be of a more abstract nature. Answer these possible questions:

1   Do you think getting to work is easier or more difficult than it used to be?

2   How have methods of transport been improved?

3   Are there any problems that have been created by new transport systems?

4   Do you think these problems can be solved?

5   What about the cost of travelling, do you think it is too high?

6   What about your ideal journey, how and where would you like to travel?

FURTHER PRACTICE FOR SPEAKING

PART 1   INTRODUCTION AND INTERVIEW

Remember that there are no right or wrong answers to the questions in Part 1. Try to relax and answer the questions naturally, giving more than a one-word answer where possible. The questions in Part 1 on page 36 are about studying. The examiner may also ask you about your job, family, hobbies and so on.

To prepare for these questions, make notes about yourself using the table below.

	Job	Family	Hobbies	Last holiday	Ambitions
Description					
How do you feel about it?					
What tense(s) can you use to talk about it?					
Any important items of vocabulary?					

Now check your answers to this exercise.

Now write one possible exam question for each of the topic areas in the table.

PART 2   INDIVIDUAL LONG TURN

You will have paper and a pencil in the exam to make notes. It is important that you use your minute of preparation time to think about and organize your answer.

Make some notes below in preparation for the talk relating to the card on page 36.

type of transport? ....
....

time? ....
....

enjoyable?...
....

improve? ....
....

Now, using your notes, talk on this topic for one to two minutes.

TEST TWO

LISTENING   approximately 30 minutes

SECTION 1   QUESTIONS 1–10

Questions 1–5

*Circle the appropriate letters **A–D**.*

Example

Hannah's Dad
    A   can hear her very well.
    (B) cannot hear her very well.
    C   wants her to move.
    D   says the line is clear.

1   How long did Hannah think it would take her to find a place to live?

    A   three weeks

    B   less than three weeks

    C   more than three weeks

    D   more than four weeks

2   There is not enough accommodation to rent because

    A   it is the end of the academic year.

    B   Hannah is a new student.

    C   the area has lots of new technology companies.

    D   the town is small.

3   £400 a month for rent is

    A   higher than Hannah has paid before.

    B   lower than Hannah has paid before.

    C   not cheap for the area.

    D   cheap for the area.

4   At the moment Hannah is living

    A   in a hostel.

    B   in a suitcase.

    C   in a hotel.

    D   in a flat.

5   Hannah's new flat

    A   is a bit noisy.

    B   is on the second floor.

    C   has two bedrooms.

    D   has a large roof terrace.

Questions 6–7

Complete Dad's note.

Hannah's address:

6........................... Whitehart Road

7........................... 9RJ

Questions 8–10

*Use **NO MORE THAN THREE WORDS** to complete each space.*

8   Hannah plans to travel to her parents' house on Friday ....

9   Hannah's Dad will return the van on ....

10   The journey time is about ....

Stop the recording when you hear 'That's the end of Section 1'.
Now check your answers to Section 1 of the test.

SECTION 2   QUESTIONS 11–20

Questions 11–14

*Circle **FOUR** letters **A–H**.*

*Which **FOUR** planned developments are mentioned?*

A	a village town hall
B	a leisure centre
C	a play area for children
D	a hospital
E	an industrial development
F	extra houses
G	a steel works
H	a motorway

Questions 15–18

*Tick Column **A** if the individual is in favour of the proposals.*

*Tick Column **B** if the individual is against the proposals.*

	A	B
Example The local farmer		✔
15 The Mayor		
16 The conservation group spokesman		
17 The local MP		
18 The local shopkeeper		

Questions 19–20

*Circle the correct letter **A–D**.*

19   Upton is

   A   close to Tartlesbury.

   B   far from Tartlesbury.

   C   connected by rail to Tartlesbury.

   D   a town with a university.

20   The College has

   A   never had a 100% success rate.

   B   had a 100% success rate this year.

   C   always been very successful.

   D   never been successful.

Stop the recording when you hear 'That's the end of Section 2'.
Now check your answers to Section 2 of the test.

SECTION 3   QUESTIONS 21–30

Questions 21–25

*Write **NO MORE THAN FOUR WORDS** or **A NUMBER** for each answer.*

21   How many essays do the students have to write?

....

22   What percentage does the written exam account for?

....

23   How many marks did Carl get for his latest essay?

....

24   How many marks did Pamela get for her latest essay?

....

25   When was the marking system explained before?

....

Questions 26–30

Complete the table below.

*Write **NO MORE THAN THREE WORDS** for each answer.*

	Carl	Pamela
Research	Very good, lots of **26** .... examples	Very good
Sources	Very sound	Very good
Organization	Very good	**29** ....
Writing style	**27**	Slightly too informal in some places
Previous essay	Disappointing, but rewrite **28**	**30** ....

Stop the recording when you hear 'That's the end of Section 3'.
Before you check your answers to Section 3 of the test, go on to page 42.

FURTHER PRACTICE FOR LISTENING SECTION 3

In the listening test some of the questions require you to understand and correctly select or identify particular facts and figures. You might be asked to complete details in sentences, a summary or notes, or select the correct details from the options you are given.

MATCHING FACTS TO FIGURES

This exercise will help you to focus on the specific information you are listening for, rather than being distracted by other numerical details which are not relevant to the task.

Listen again to the first part of Section 3 and match the figures and quantities (a–g) below to the items they refer to (1–6). You will not need to use all of the answers.

Stop the recording when Dr Woodham says 'any questions or comments?'

1   number of essays

2   maximum marks for each essay

3   total essay marks each year

4   contribution of essays to final degree

5   contribution Carl's essay has made to his final grade

6   contribution Pamela's essay has made to her final grade

a   7%

b   9%

c   30%

d   50%

e   5

f   20

g   100

Now check your answers to this exercise. When you have done so, listen again to Section 3 of the test and decide whether you wish to change any of the answers you gave. Then check your answers to Section 3 of the test.

SECTION 4   QUESTIONS 31–40

Questions 31–35

*Circle the correct letters **A–D**.*

31   The total number of lectures mentioned by the lecturer is

    A   ten.

    B   thirteen.

    C   six.

    D   eight.

32   The lunch break of the average British worker is

    A   on the increase.

    B   shorter than it used to be.

    C   36 minutes.

    D   precisely 30 minutes.

33   Which graph shows the change as regards sick leave?

    A 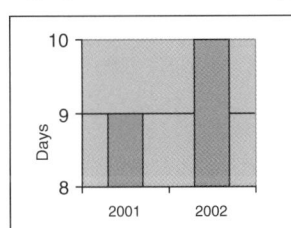   **B**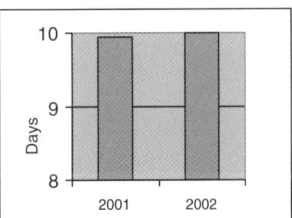

    C 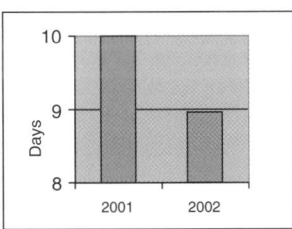   **D**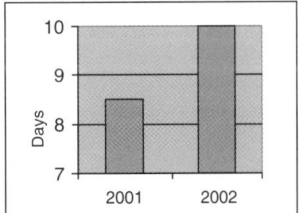

34   There will be another lecture on stress in work and study

    A   given by Professor Butt.

    B   on the calendar.

    C   in about a fortnight.

    D   in a week's time.

35   Which of the following is mentioned?

    A   Most workers say they do not take all their holidays.

    B   Under half of the workers say they do not take all their holidays.

    C   Employers do not believe workers.

    D   About a third of healthy workers take days off sick.

Questions 36–39

Complete the table below.

Write NO MORE THAN THREE WORDS for each answer.

Student's Notes

Employees	*now working* **36** .... *physically and mentally*
Productivity	*up in many* **37** ....
In 2002, local car plant	*vehicles per employee on rise to* **38** ....
Car industry	*once thought to be* **39** ....

Question 40

Choose the correct letter A–D.

40   Dr Butt asks those students to see him who

  A   want to work at the plant.

  B   have chosen to do the project.

  C   want to write extra essays.

  D   are new.

Stop the recording when you hear 'That's the end of Section 4'.
Before you check your answers to Section 4 of the test, go on to pages 45–46.

FURTHER PRACTICE FOR LISTENING SECTION 4

MATCHING FIGURES TO CONTEXTS

It is important to be clear about the context in which facts and figures are mentioned, and not to jump to conclusions when you hear a number or a detail in the recording.

Example

Dr Charles Butt will be giving

A   ten lectures.

B   three lectures.

C   thirteen lectures.

D   six to eight lectures.

Answer: A

The other figures (B–D) are all either mentioned or can be deduced from what you hear in this section of the listening test, but they do not answer this question.

The following exercise will help you to focus on what the numerical data mentioned refers to.

*Listen again to Section 4 and choose the correct answer **a–d**. More than one answer may be correct in each case.*

Stop the recording when Dr Butt says 'considered to be collapsing'.

1   From six to eight is

    a   the number of extra lectures.

    b   the time of the extra lectures.

    c   the number of outside speakers.

    d   the number of vacant places on the course.

2   Twenty-seven minutes is

    a   the average lunch break now.

    b   last year's average lunch break.

    c   the shortest lunch break ever.

    d   not long enough for lunch.

3   Nine out of ten is

    a   the average figure for sick leave.

    b   the number of workers who consider stress at work to be a problem.

    c   the number of employers who are stressed.

    d   the number of lectures dealing with stress.

4   The proportion of days off sick that workers take but bosses do not think are genuine is

    a   30%.

    b   just below 50%.

    c   two-thirds.

    d   between one- and two-thirds.

5   At the local car plant, 30% is

    a   current productivity.

    b   average productivity.

    c   the productivity rise in 2001.

    d   the expected increase in productivity in 2002.

Now check your answers to this exercise. When you have done so, listen again to Section 4 of the test and decide whether you wish to change any of the answers you gave. Then check your answers to Section 4 of the test.

ACADEMIC READING   60 minutes

READING PASSAGE 1

*You should spend about 20 minutes on **Questions 1–15** which are based on Reading Passage 1 below.*

ADAM'S WINE

A   Water is the giver and, at the same time, the taker of life. It covers most of the surface of the planet we live on and features large in the development of the human race. On present predictions, it is an element that is set to assume even greater significance.

B   Throughout history, water has had a huge impact on our lives. Humankind has always had a rather ambiguous relationship with water, on the one hand receiving enormous benefit from it, not just as a drinking source, but as a provider of food and a means whereby to travel and to trade. But forced to live close to water in order to survive and to develop, the relationship has not always been peaceful or beneficial. In fact, it has been quite the contrary. What has essentially been a necessity for survival has turned out in many instances to have a very destructive and life-threatening side.

C   Through the ages, great floods alternated with long periods of drought have assaulted people and their environment, hampering their fragile fight for survival. The dramatic changes to the environment that are now a feature of our daily news are not exactly new: fields that were once lush and fertile are now barren; lakes and rivers that were once teeming with life are now long gone; savannah has been turned to desert. What perhaps is new is our naïve wonder when faced with the forces of nature.

D   Today, we are more aware of climatic changes around the world. Floods in far-flung places are instant news for the whole world. Perhaps these events make us feel better as we face the destruction of our own property by floods and other natural disasters.

E   In 2002, many parts of Europe suffered severe flood damage running into billions of euros. Properties across the continent collapsed into the sea as waves pounded the coastline wreaking havoc with sea defences. But it was not just the seas. Rivers swollen by heavy rains and by the effects of deforestation carried large volumes of water that wrecked many communities.

F   Building stronger and more sophisticated river defences against flooding is the expensive short-term answer. There are simpler ways. Planting trees in highland areas, not just in Europe but in places like the Himalayas, to protect people living in low-lying regions like the Ganges Delta, is a cheaper and more attractive solution. Progress is already being made in convincing countries that the emission of carbon dioxide and other greenhouse gases is causing considerable damage to the environment. But more effort is needed in this direction.

G   And the future? If we are to believe the forecasts, it is predicted that two-thirds of the world population will be without fresh water by 2025. But for a growing number of regions of the world the future is already with us. While some areas are devastated by flooding, scarcity of water in many other places is causing conflict. The state of Texas in the United States of America is suffering a shortage of water with the Rio Grande failing to reach the Gulf of Mexico for the first time in 50 years in the spring of 2002, pitting region against region as they vie for water sources. With many parts of the globe running dry through drought and increased water consumption, there is now talk of water being the new oil.

H   Other doom-laden estimates suggest that, while tropical areas will become drier and uninhabitable, coastal regions and some low-lying islands will in all probability be submerged by the sea as the polar ice caps melt. Popular exotic destinations now visited by countless tourists will become no-go areas. Today's holiday hotspots of southern Europe and elsewhere will literally become hotspots – too hot to live in or visit. With the current erratic behaviour of the weather, it is difficult not to subscribe to such despair.

I   Some might say that this despondency is ill-founded, but we have had ample proof that there is something not quite right with the climate. Many parts of the world have experienced devastating flooding. As the seasons revolve, the focus of the destruction moves from one continent to another. The impact on the environment is alarming and the cost to life depressing. It is a picture to which we will need to become accustomed.

Questions 1–8

Reading Passage 1 has nine paragraphs labelled **A–I**.

*Choose the most suitable headings for paragraphs **B–I** from the list of headings below.*

*Write the appropriate numbers (**i–xiii**) in boxes 1–8 on your answer sheet.*

One of the headings has been done for you as an example.

Note: There are more headings than paragraphs, so you will not use all of them.

List of Headings

i   Environmental change has always been with us

ii   The scarcity of water

iii Rivers and seas cause damage

iv   Should we be despondent? Or realistic?

v   Disasters caused by the climate make us feel better

vi   Water, the provider of food

vii What is water?

viii How to solve flooding

ix   Far-flung flooding

x   Humans' relationship with water

xi   The destructive force of water in former times

xii Flooding in the future

xiii A pessimistic view of the future

Example	Paragraph **A**	*Answer* **vii**

1   Paragraph **B**

2   Paragraph **C**

3   Paragraph **D**

4   Paragraph **E**

5   Paragraph **F**

6   Paragraph **G**

7   Paragraph **H**

8   Paragraph **I**

Questions 9–15

*Choose the appropriate letters **A–D** and write them in boxes 9–15 on your answer sheet.*

9 The writer believes that water

    A is gradually becoming of greater importance.

    B will have little impact on our lives in future.

    C is something we will need more than anything else.

    D will have even greater importance in our lives in the future.

10 Humankind's relationship with water has been

    A two-sided.

    B one-sided.

    C purely one of great benefit.

    D fairly frightening.

11 The writer suggests that

    A we are in awe of the news we read and see on TV every day.

    B change to the environment leaves us speechless.

    C we should not be in awe of the news we read and see on TV every day.

    D our surprise at the environmental change brought about by nature is something new.

12 According to the text, planting trees

    A has to be co-ordinated internationally.

    B is more expensive than building sea and river defences.

    C is a less expensive answer to flooding than building river defences.

    D is not an answer to the problem of flooding in all regions.

13 By 2025, it is projected that

    A at least half the world population will have fresh water.

    B the majority of the world population will have fresh water.

    C one-third of the world population will have fresh water.

    D fresh water will only be available to half of the world population.

14   According to the text, in the future low-lying islands

    A   will still be habitable.

    B   will not be under water.

    C   are likely to be under water.

    D   will probably not be under water.

15   According to the writer,

    A   people do not need to get used to environmental damage.

    B   people will need to get used to climate changes that cause environmental damage.

    C   people are now more used to environmental damage than they have been in the past.

    D   the general despondency about environmental changes is ill-founded.

Before you check your answers to Reading Passage 1, go on to pages 52–54.

FURTHER PRACTICE FOR READING PASSAGE 1

MULTIPLE-CHOICE QUESTIONS

- Remember to read the first part of the sentence each time you read the alternatives. It is easy to forget what the original stem says when you get to option D.
- To help you concentrate, use a piece of paper to cover the questions and then reveal the alternatives one at a time.
- Learn to look for distractors (options which may seem to be correct, but on closer inspection are not, perhaps because they are only partly true, or because the information does not actually appear in the text).

The questions below will help you to make sure that you have chosen the correct answers for questions 9–15 on Reading Passage 1.

Question 9 *Look at paragraph A.*

1   The writer mentions the importance of water. Where?

   ....

2   Does the writer say anything about the effect of water on our lives in the future?

   ....

3   Does the writer compare water to anything else?

   ....

Question 10 *Look at paragraph B.*

1   Which word is closest to the meaning of 'ambiguous'?

   a   not clear

   b   obvious

   c   peculiar

   d   striking

2   Does the writer show that humankind has had a relationship with water?

   ....

3   How many aspects does this relationship have?

   ....

4   If there is one aspect, what is it? If two, what are they?

   ....

Question 11 Look at paragraph C.

1   Does the writer mention anything about news?

      ....

2   Does the writer mention the source of the news?

      ....

3   Does the writer say anything about the effect of environmental change on us?

      ....

4   Does the text mention anything about our attitude to the changes brought about by nature?

      ....

Question 12 Look at paragraph F.

1   Does the paragraph mention solutions to flooding?

      ....

2   Does the paragraph mention international co-ordination?

      ....

3   Is planting trees compared with anything else?

      ....

4   If it is, which is the cheaper option?

      ....

Question 13 Look at paragraph G.

1   What does the expression 'be without fresh water' mean?

      ....

2   How many people will have fresh water by 2025? A third or two-thirds?

      ....

Question 14 Look at paragraph H.

1   Does the paragraph mention what will happen to low-lying islands in the future?

....

2   If so, what will happen?

....

3   Is the writer's prediction about the future certain or probable?

....

Question 15 Look at paragraph I.

1   Where does the writer state his or her conclusion to the paragraph?

....

2   Where does the writer state what other people think? Which words show you?

....

3   Does the writer compare people being accustomed to environmental damage now and in the past?

....

*Now check your answers to these exercises. When you have done so, decide whether you wish
to change any of your answers to Reading Passage 1. Then check your answers to Reading
Passage 1.*

READING PASSAGE 2

*You should spend about 20 minutes on **Questions 16–30** which are based on Reading Passage 2 below.*

Is it any wonder that there are teacher shortages? Daily, the press carries reports of schools going on four-day weeks simply because they cannot recruit enough teachers. But why? There is no straightforward answer. For a start, fewer students are entering teacher-training courses when they leave school. But can you blame young people after the barracking faced by the teaching profession in the UK over the last decade? The attack, relentless in the extreme, has been on several fronts. Government inspectors, by accident or design, have been feeding the media a constant stream of negative information about the teaching establishments in this country. Teachers also come in for a lot of flak from politicians. And the government wonders why there are problems in schools.

The government's obvious contempt for the teaching profession was recently revealed by one of the most powerful people in government when she referred to schools as 'bog standard comprehensives'. Hardly the sort of comment to inspire parents or careers advisers seeking to direct young people's future. Would you want to spend your working life in a dead-end profession? The government doesn't seem to want you to either.

On the administrative side, most teachers are weighed down by an increasing flow of bureaucracy. Cynicism would have me believe that this stops teachers from fomenting dissent as they are worn out by useless administrative exercises. Most teachers must then also be cynics!

Teacher bashing has, unfortunately, spread to youngsters in schools as the recent catalogue of physical attacks on teachers will testify. If grown-ups have no respect for the teaching profession, young people can hardly be expected to think any differently. The circle is then squared when, as well as experienced, competent teachers being driven out of the profession by the increased pressure and stress, fewer students are applying for teacher-training courses.

Increased salaries are certainly welcome, but they are not the complete answer to a sector in crisis. Addressing the standing of the profession in the eyes of the public is crucial to encourage experienced teachers to remain in the classroom and to make it an attractive career option for potential teachers once again.

It might also be a good idea for the relevant ministers to go on a fact-finding mission and find out from teachers in schools, rather than relying overmuch on advisers, as to what changes could be brought about to improve the quality of the education service. Initiatives in the educational field surprisingly come from either politicians who know little about classroom practice or educational theorists who know even less, but are more dangerous because they work in the rarefied air of universities largely ignorant of classroom practice.

Making sure that nobody without recent classroom experience is employed as a teacher-trainer at any tertiary institution would further enhance the teaching profession. If someone does not have practical experience in the classroom, they cannot in all seriousness propound theories about it. Instead of being given sabbaticals to write books or papers, lecturers in teacher-training establishments should be made to spend a year at the blackboard or, these days, the whiteboard. This would give them practical insights into current classroom practice. Student teachers could then be given the chance to come and watch the specialists in the classroom: a much more worthwhile experience than the latter sitting thinking up ideas far removed from the classroom. Then we would have fewer initiatives like the recent government proposal to teach thinking in school. Prima facie, this is a laudable recommendation. But, as any practising teacher will tell you, this is done in every class. Perhaps someone needs to point out to the academic who thought up the scheme that the wheel has been around for some time.

In the educational field, there is surprisingly constant tension between the educational theorists and government officials on the one hand, who would like to see teachers marching in unison to some greater Utopian abstraction and, on the other, practising teachers. Any experienced classroom practitioner knows that the series of initiatives on teaching and learning that successive governments have tried to foist on schools and colleges do not work.

Questions 16–22

Complete the summary below of the first four paragraphs of Reading Passage 2.

*Use **ONE WORD** from the passage for each answer.*

Write your answers in boxes 16–22 on your answer sheet.

Is it surprising that there is a **16**............... of teachers? Schools do not have enough teachers, but what are the reasons for this? To begin with, fewer students are going into **17**............... courses after finishing school. But this is not young people's fault. The **18**............... of teaching has been under constant attack over the last ten years. The government's lack of respect for the profession is **19**............... . Moreover, administratively, the flow of bureaucracy is **20**............... . Even pupils in schools have no respect for those who teach them, as a **21**............... series of assaults on teachers shows. The growing strain and stress means that, as well as fewer applications for teacher-training courses, teachers who have experience and are **22**............... are also being driven out.

Questions 23–29

Do the following statements agree with the views of the writer in Reading Passage 2?

In boxes 23–29 on your answer sheet write

    YES   *if the statement agrees with the claims of the writer*
    NO   *if the statement contradicts the claims of the writer*
    NOT GIVEN *if it is impossible to say what the writer thinks about this*

> *Example*
>   The four-day week in schools is caused by a lack of teachers.
> *Answer*
>   Yes

23   More students are entering teacher-training courses.

24   The government is right to be surprised that there are problems in schools.

25   Teachers are too weighed down by administrative duties to stir up trouble.

26   All teachers are cynics.

27   Politicians are not as dangerous as educational theorists, who know even less than the former about educational theory.

28   Any experienced classroom practitioner knows that the initiatives on teaching and learning that governments have tried to impose on schools do not work.

29   The government's attitude with regard to teachers is of great interest to the general public.

Question 30

*Choose the appropriate letter **A–D** and write it in box 30 on your answer sheet.*

30   Which one of the following is the most suitable title for the passage?

    A   Politicians and teachers.

    B   A profession undervalued.

    C   Recruitment difficulties in the teaching profession.

    D   Teacher-training needs improvement.

Before you check your answers to Reading Passage 2, go on to page 58.

FURTHER PRACTICE FOR READING PASSAGE 2

SUMMARY COMPLETION

- The summary will be a completion of part or all of the passage so check carefully which part the summary refers to.
- The words used in the summary may not always be the same as those in the original phrase. Look for synonyms of key words in the text.
- All the words which you need are in the original text, but their grammatical form may need to be changed (see below).

The questions below will help you to make sure that you have chosen the correct answers for questions 16–22 on Reading Passage 2.

1   Below is a list of the grammatical items that you need to complete spaces 16–22 in the test. Choose one for each blank space. Items can be used more than once and you may not need all of them.

16   ....

17   ....

18   ....

19   ....

20   ....

21   ....

22   ....

List of grammatical items
a singular noun
b plural noun
c adjective
d adverb
e verb

2   In summary completion exercises, parts of the original passage are often paraphrased in the summary. Find the word or phrase in the summary that means the same as the words or phrases below taken from Reading Passage 2:

Paragraph 1

1   any wonder   ....

2   entering   ....

3   barracking   ....

4   decade   ....

Paragraph 2

5   contempt   ....

Paragraph 4

6   teachers   ....

7   catalogue   ....

8   pressure   ....

Now check your answers to these exercises. When you have done so, decide whether you wish to change any of your answers to Reading Passage 2. Then check your answers to Reading Passage 2.

READING PASSAGE 3

*You should spend about 20 minutes on **Questions 31–40** which are based on Reading Passage 3 below.*

EVA HESSE
Three Pieces Plus...

The Guggenheim Art Gallery, New York.

Image courtesy of The Estate of Eva Hesse, Galerie Hauser & Wirth, Zurich.

I n one corner of the room is a mass of tangled rope suspended from the ceiling with some sections dangling to the floor; the first of three encountered pieces of work that have a resounding impact on the viewing public. It stops one in one's tracks: how dare it be there – this mess of nothing! It is like arranged chaos: that is, the confused mixture of varying sizes of rope, dipped in latex, looks as though it might collapse in a heap on the floor at any moment. At the same time, it is held up and in place by a series of fine wires and hooks, giving it a strange sense of ... order. A deliberate challenge to the forces of gravity. It is a shambles. It makes one laugh. It is play. It is drawing in the air! Maybe it can move or dance about! Yet, it is hardly there, like something imagined.

The materials are cheap and disposable. Impermanent, like ... the people looking at it. But it is very definitely present! It has a presence. You can see that people want to walk into it and become a part of it – but alas! The gallery guard is hovering nearby.

To the left of this piece, running along the wall, in two rows on top of each other, is a long series of lid-less boxes. They are mounted at average nose height and are made of fibreglass which gives them a shiny, almost moist, appearance. They are the colour of murky water, absorbing the gallery light with an opacity similar to that of mucus or tree gum. They look as though they might be soft and malleable to touch, with their irregular edges and non-conforming sides. This gives the overall impression that they could fall in on themselves or slide down the wall. The structure is puzzlingly familiar, similar to things in the world, and yet it is not like anything in particular.

In the adjacent corner is the third piece, consisting of a collection of nine cylindrical open-ended objects, slit part way from end to end. They give the appearance of being randomly placed – some lying, some leaning on the wall or on each other – all

Image courtesy of The Estate of Eva Hesse, Galerie Hauser & Wirth, Zurich.

seeming somehow to be related. Like the boxes, they are a multiple of each other. Made of fibreglass with a shiny surface they look almost like abandoned pods that had once been alive. The associations seem to jump around in one's head, running between sensations of delight and pleasure, violence and discomfort.

One has to bend down to be with them more. Driven by the desire to physically interact, one is almost forced to stoop further so that one can touch, or indeed taste, this intriguing surface; but no, the guard is there.

The visual language apparent in these artworks is unfamiliar, as is the artist, Eva Hesse. Her work is as exciting as it is disturbing. For many, Hesse's sculpture refers essentially to the body. This, perhaps, does not seem surprising when it is in relation to the body that women are generally assessed. Hesse died of a brain tumour in 1970 at the age of 34. It must be an inescapable inevitability, therefore, that her work was read in the context of its time where it has, until recently, been largely abandoned.

Given the influence of feminism on our cultural consciousness since that period, it seems paramount that we avoid, or at the very least attempt to avoid, those dramatic facts about her life and family history. We may then be freed from a limited and narrow translation of her art.

Hesse's work is much more ambiguous and funny than some rather literal readings would have us believe. Perhaps it is precisely because her use of metaphor in her work is so subtle that it escapes the one-line definitions we so love to employ.

We are now, more than ever, hungry for the cult of 'personality'. While Hesse and others before and since can more than fill that demand, we seem in danger of focusing on the life of the artist and not on the life of the art.

When looking at Hesse's sculpture, drawings and paintings, the most interesting and challenging aspects lie just there – *within the work*. And this must be the starting point for any interpretation, not her complex life or untimely death.

Questions 31–36

Do the following statements agree with the writer's opinion in Reading Passage 3?

In boxes 31–36 on your answer sheet write

YES   *if the statement agrees with the writer's opinion*
NO   *if the statement contradicts the writer's opinion*
NOT GIVEN   *if there is no information about the writer's opinion*

Example	*Answer*
The Guggenheim Art Gallery is in New York.	Yes

31   The first piece of Hesse's art has little effect on visitors to the gallery.

32   The order inherent in the first piece of Hesse's art is essential to the understanding of her work.

33   The second piece of art by Hesse is inferior in several significant ways to the first.

34   The second piece by Hesse has several design faults that attract the public.

35   The third piece of work arouses different emotions.

36   Of the three pieces of Hesse's work described, the first is the writer's favourite.

Questions 37–40

*Choose the appropriate letters **A–D** and write them in boxes 37–40 on your answer sheet.*

37 According to the writer, Eva Hesse

    A is not a well-known artist.

    B is very familiar, as is her work.

    C is not a good artist.

    D is strongly attracted by visual language.

38 The writer concludes that

    A Hesse's work is timeless.

    B the understanding of Hesse's work has until recently been interpreted only in the context of its time.

    C Hesse's work is a product of her time and is not relevant to the modern world.

    D Hesse's work is easy to read.

39 The writer thinks that it is .... to define Hesse's work.

    A not difficult

    B essential

    C not important

    D not easy

40 In the present climate,

    A we may lose sight of Hesse's art and focus on her life.

    B personality is very important.

    C art cults are in vogue.

    D we may lose sight of Hesse's life and focus on her art.

Now check your answers to Reading Passage 3.

ACADEMIC WRITING   60 minutes

TASK 1

You should spend about 20 minutes on this task.

The bar chart below shows the results of a survey conducted by a personnel department at a major company. The survey was carried out on two groups of workers: those aged from 18–30 and those aged 45–60, and shows factors affecting their work performance.

Write a report for a university lecturer describing the information below.

Write at least 150 words.

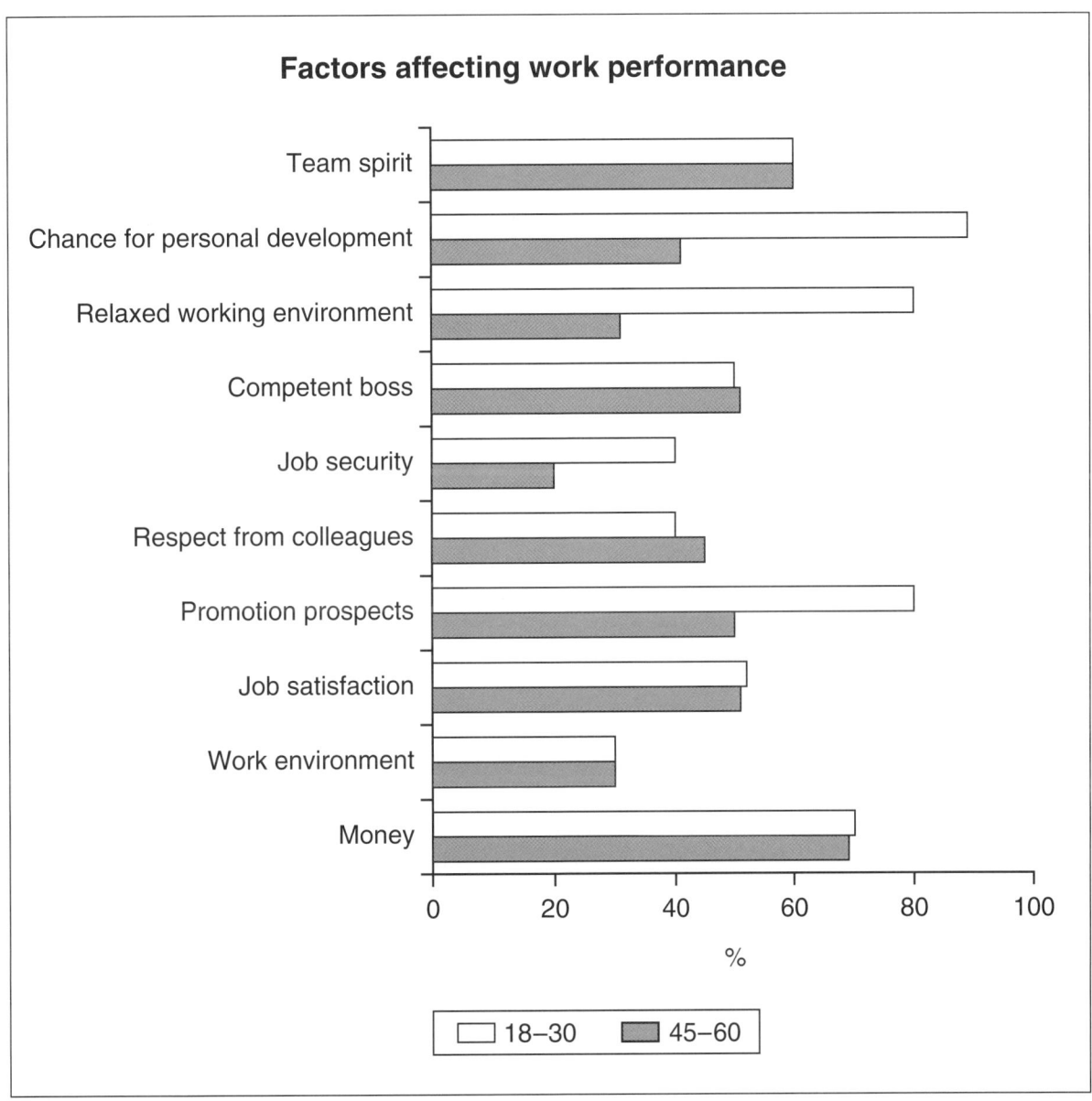

Before you write your answer to Task 1, go on to pages 64–65.

FURTHER PRACTICE FOR TASK 1

1   *When working with a chart it is important to think carefully about the information it presents and how you will organize your answer. Look at the chart in Task 1 on page 63 and answer the following questions:*

a   Will your report be subjective or objective?

   ....

b   It is easier to describe and compare items in smaller groups. Can you organize the elements on the vertical axis into groups?

   ....

c   You will need to report what people say in answer to survey questions. What other words or phrases can you use instead of 'said it was' in the following sentence?

   Regarding team spirit, 60% of the workers in each category <u>said it was</u> an important factor.

   ....

   ....

d   What other ways can you compare and contrast the data below?

   Job security was much less important for the older group than the younger, at 20% and 40% respectively.

   ....

   ....

2   *Look at the chart on page 63 and complete the sentences below using a word for each blank space. The sentences are not in any particular order and some of the information is expressed twice but in a different way. In some cases there may be more than one suitable answer.*

   The missing items are in the box on page 65. First, try to complete the sentences without looking at the box.

> *Example*
>   The bar chart ..... *shows/illustrates* ..... the results of a .... *survey* .... of
>   workers at a major company on what elements affect how .... *well* .... they work.
>
>   Note how the phrase 'how well they work' paraphrases 'work performance' in the test.

a   The .... was carried .... on two groups of workers,

   ....: those aged between 18 and 30 and those aged between 45 and 60.

b   .... over 80% of workers in the 18 to 30-year-old group considered the chance for

   personal development to be the .... important factor, it was .... as

   influential by only 40% of the older group.

c   A relaxed working environment, promotion prospects and chance for personal development were

   .... the greatest .... by the younger of the two groups, at 80% or

   more of the poll sample. By .... , the 45 to 60-year-olds rated these factors much

   less at 30%, 50% and 40% ....

d   Job security was considered much .... important for the older group than the younger, at 20% as .... to 40%.

e   The work environment mattered .... to each group at 30%.

f   As .... team spirit, 60% of the workers polled mentioned it as being an important factor.

g   The most .... feature of the chart is the similarity in the judgement of both groups in six out of ten factors.

h   In six out of ten items the two groups more or less agreed, while for the other items they .... in opinion by varying degrees.

i   Both groups agreed .... the importance of the work environment in influencing their performance, with around 30% of workers mentioning it in each group.

j   The elements can be arranged into two .... categories, namely, those which are valued as equally or almost equally important by both groups of workers and those where there is difference in importance.

equally	respectively	namely	on	distinct	while	cited	most	given
importance	opposed	regards	striking	survey	differed	contrast	less	out

3   Now write your own answer to Task 1 on page 63. You may use some of the sentences or phrases above, but you will need to make changes to form a well-structured report. When you have finished writing your report, compare it to the authentic student answer in the key on page 141.

Is your finished answer to Task 1 an appropriate length? How many lines of your usual handwriting represents 150/160 words?

TASK 2

You should spend about 40 minutes on this task.

Write about the following topic:

> *Too much attention is paid to and too much money is spent on keeping pets, while people throughout the world are starving.*
>
> - *Discuss the arguments for and against keeping pets.*
> - *To what extent do you agree?*

Give reasons for your answer and include any relevant examples from your own knowledge or experience.

Write at least 250 words.

Before you write your answer to Task 2, go on to page 67.

FURTHER PRACTICE FOR TASK 2

1   *It is important to structure your essay well and avoid repetition. Look at this model introductory paragraph for Task 2. For paragraph two, make choices to continue the text in the most suitable way by choosing one option from each of the columns A, B and C for numbers 1–6.*

> To some people, too much money is spent on and too much attention is paid to pet animals, while many human beings throughout the world are starving. Others feel, however, that keeping animals as pets is of great benefit.

	A	B	C
1	Some people are of the opinion that too much money	People feel that more and more money	People are of the opinion that more and more money
2	is now being spent on animals	is spent on dogs, cats, birds and other luxuries, and so on	is now being spent on a variety of pets such as dogs, cats, birds, and so on
3	and that it is wrong to treat dogs like children.	and that it is wrong to treat dogs like children when many people are dying of hunger.	and that it is wrong to treat them like children when there are many people, especially children, dying of hunger.
4	In richer countries pet animals are better fed.	For example, in richer countries animals are better fed than the poor people.	For example, in many rich countries domestic animals are given better food to eat than poor people.
5	A group believes that human beings are important	Those who hold this point of view would argue that human beings are more important than animals	They feel human beings are more important
6	and therefore deserve to be better fed.	and they feel they deserve to be better looked after.	and as such, deserve to be fed.

2   *Now, using the notes below, finish the essay in your own words.*

Paragraph 3
others say – pets beneficial
help adults/children relate to
nature & treat animals better –
add own experience

Paragraph 4
pets = companion for
lonely/elderly
e.g. dogs need exercise =
1) healthy
2) meeting people

Conclusion
my personal view
and why

When you have finished writing the essay, compare it to the model and authentic student answers in the key on page 141.

SPEAKING 11–14 minutes

PART 1 INTRODUCTION AND INTERVIEW (4–5 MINUTES)

In this part of the examination you will first be asked your name and then you will be asked questions about yourself. Answer these possible questions:

1 Is English important in your chosen career?

2 What do you hope to do in the future?

3 Have you given up anything you used to do in your free time? If so, what?

4 Which other hobbies or sports would you like to try?

5 Do you share similar interests with your friends?

PART 2 INDIVIDUAL LONG TURN (3–4 MINUTES)

You will have to talk about the topic on the card for one to two minutes. You have one minute to think about what you are going to say and make some notes to help you if you wish.

> Describe the job or career you have, or hope to have.
>
> You should say:
>
> - what the job is
> - what it involves
> - why you chose it
>
> and explain why it is rewarding.

Now look at the Further Practice section on page 69.

PART 3 TWO-WAY DISCUSSION (4–5 MINUTES)

In this part of the exam, the examiner will discuss a topic with you. The topic is usually related in some way to the topic in Part 2, but the questions will be of a more abstract nature. Answer these possible questions:

1 What do most people consider as important when deciding on a job or career?

2 In modern life a lot of people work too hard. What are the effects of this?

3 How could the problems of overworking be avoided?

4 At what age do you think people should retire from work?

5 Do you think this should be the same for all jobs?

6 How has technology changed the way that people work?

7 What further changes in the way people work do you think we will see in the future?

Now look at the Further Practice section on page 69.

FURTHER PRACTICE FOR SPEAKING

PART 2   INDIVIDUAL LONG TURN

In this section you have the chance to use a variety of grammatical structures and vocabulary.

In the text below think of as many alternatives as possible for the underlined words in the sample answer. To achieve a higher grade in the speaking test avoid repetition and try to use more sophisticated vocabulary, not just the easiest word that you can think of.

> I work as a doctor in a busy practice in the centre of a <u>large</u> city in the south of the country. My work is very <u>hard</u> because it involves not only seeing patients when they have an appointment at the surgery where I work, but also making home visits and helping patients who are unable to come to the surgery. I chose to be a doctor <u>because</u> I enjoy contact with people and it is <u>nice</u> to know that you are doing something <u>good</u> in your job. Being a doctor is <u>very</u> rewarding because patients are so <u>pleased</u> when their medical problems are solved. It is great to know that I am making a real difference and <u>helping</u> people to become fit and well again.

Now check your answers to this exercise.

Thinking carefully about the vocabulary you use, describe your job using the card on page 68.

PART 3   TWO-WAY DISCUSSION

In Part 3 of the test you are asked to give your opinion on various aspects of a topic. It is important to use a variety of different phrases to introduce your point of view, for example:

In my opinion, ...	From my point of view, ...	If you ask me, ...
In my view, ...	As far as I am concerned, ...	It seems to me (that) ...
To my mind, ...	I suppose/imagine (that) ...	I think/believe (that) ...

Using the phrases in the box and the ideas below, expand your answers to Part 3 of the test on page 68.

1   salary, job satisfaction, working hours, workplace

2   mental stress, physical illness, breakdown of family relationships

3   laws limiting the working week, job-sharing, compulsory time off

4   the situation in your country, men compared to women

5   mentally demanding compared to physically demanding jobs, e.g. lawyer/builder or politician/athlete

6   some things better, e.g. communication (e-mail), computer programs, but others worse, e.g. lack of personal contact, problems when systems fail

7   working from home, more communication through computers or video screens, more work done by machines of all kinds, shorter working hours, job-sharing, flexi-time

TEST THREE

LISTENING   approximately 30 minutes

SECTION 1   QUESTIONS 1–10

Questions 1–5

*Write **NO MORE THAN THREE WORDS** for each answer.*

Example	*Answer*
How long has Caroline been waiting?	five minutes

1   What does Matt suggest they do?

   ....

2   In which month is the party going to take place?

   ....

3   Where is Nikki?

   ....

4   How long is Matt is going to be away for?

   ....

5   What day of the week is the party going to be held?

   ....

Questions 6–10

*Circle the correct letters **A–C**.*

6   The location of
   Nikki's house
   on the map is

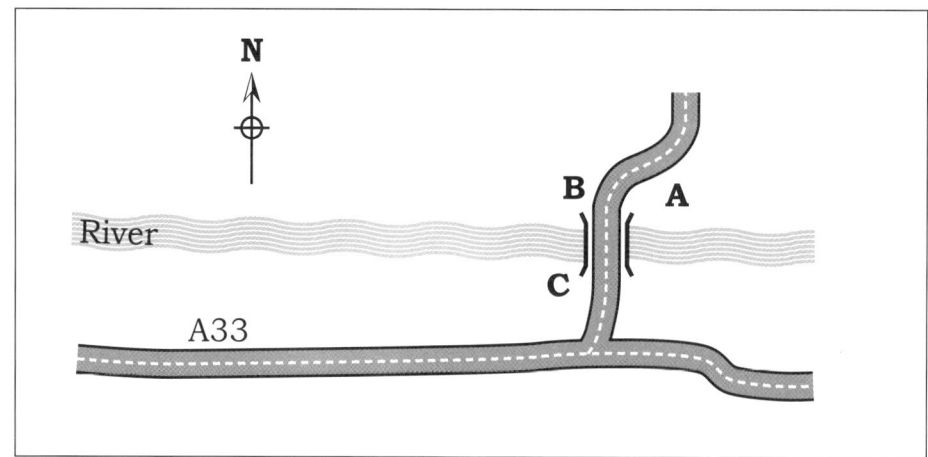

7   The house has

    A   a bridge over the river.

    B   a large swimming pool.

    C   gardens leading down to the river.

8   The address is

    A   93 Western Road.

    B   39 West Road.

    C   93 West Road.

9   The telephone number is

    A   477113.

    B   447130.

    C   477130.

10   Each person has to give

    A   ten pounds.

    B   refreshments.

    C   a barbecue.

Stop the recording when you hear 'That's the end of Section 1'.
Now check your answers to Section 1 of the test.

SECTION 2   QUESTIONS 11–20

Questions 11–13

*Write **NO MORE THAN TWO WORDS** for each answer.*

Philosophy Department – Tutor's responsibilities

Main function	Personal matters	Appointments	Urgent matters
To provide help with academic work in the philosophy course.	To refer students to other support services in the university, which **11**..................... from counselling to welfare.	To make an appointment, students should write their name in a time slot in **12**..................... on the door.	To speak to the tutor students should **13**..................... between sessions.

Questions 14–19

*Circle the correct letter **A–C**.*

14   Tutorials are

    A   obligatory.

    B   voluntary.

    C   once every two weeks.

15   Tutorial registers in the Philosophy department

    A   started last year.

    B   are not taken.

    C   will start this year.

16   Most students

    A   were very annoyed by people arriving late.

    B   were fairly annoyed by people arriving late.

    C   did not like exit questionnaires.

17   In the tutorial, there will be a review of the lectures

    A   by the tutor.

    B   for the previous week.

    C   by a visiting lecturer.

18   Preparation for the tutorial each week may include

    A   preparing an outline.

    B   writing an essay.

    C   in-depth analysis.

19   Continuous assessment grades do not include

    A   essays.

    B   project work.

    C   mini-presentations.

Question 20

*Write **NO MORE THAN THREE WORDS** for the answer.*

The tutor hopes tutorial activities will have an impact on students' ....

Stop the recording when you hear 'That's the end of Section 2'.
Before you check your answers to Section 2 of the test, go on to page 73.

FURTHER PRACTICE FOR LISTENING SECTION 2

GRAMMATICAL CHANGES

Some listening exercises require you to complete gapped sentences with a maximum number of words. The sentence you hear may not be exactly the same as the one you are asked to complete. You need to extract the information when you hear it and, if necessary, change the form of the word or phrase before you complete the answer.

The following exercise will help you to practise changing the form of words to fit the grammar of a sentence. Before listening, try to identify the part(s) of speech needed for each space below.

Now listen to Section 2 again and complete each sentence using no more than two words.

Stop the recording when you hear 'Does that answer your question?'

1   The .... help the tutor is able to give is with academic work.

2   There is .... of appointment times on the tutor's door.

3   In the Philosophy department all the tutors have made .... to keep registers.

4   In tutorials, the philosophy lectures will ....

5   As regards planning for the tutorial discussion, students should rely primarily on their

     ....

6   Students will be expected to .... each week for the tutorials.

7   All graded essays and project work .... towards continuous assessment grades.

Now check your answers to this exercise. When you have done so, listen again to Section 2 of the test and decide whether you wish to change any of the answers you gave. Then check your answers to Section 2 of the test.

SECTION 3   QUESTIONS 21–30

Questions 21–23

Circle the correct letter A–D.

21   The students are discussing

    A   one essay of 1,500 words.

    B   four essays of 1,500 words.

    C   one essay of 5,000 words.

    D   one essay of 5,000–6,000 words.

22   Which of the following can be included in the assignment?

    A   Dr Brightwell's notes

    B   tables and graphs, but not charts

    C   tables, graphs and charts

    D   social science books

23   What has to be handed in to Dr Brightwell in two weeks' time?

    A   data for the graphs

    B   a questionnaire in draft form

    C   a completed questionnaire

    D   collected information

Question 24

Write NO MORE THAN TWO WORDS or A NUMBER.

The question limit on the questionnaire is ....

Questions 25–30

Match the points below to the speaker.

*Circle **M** for Mark or **A** for Anne.*

25 Forty questions will be enough.	M	A
26 The questions should be simple.	M	A
27 The subject of the questionnaire will be how active students are.	M	A
28 The questionnaires do not need to have names.	M	A
29 Twenty to twenty-five questions should be written by both of them.	M	A
30 The layout of the questionnaire can be played with.	M	A

Stop the recording when you hear 'That's the end of Section 3'.

Before you check your answers to Section 3 of the test, go on to page 76.

FURTHER PRACTICE FOR LISTENING SECTION 3

IDENTIFYING SPEAKERS

In some questions you are required to identify attitudes, opinions or statements given or made by one or more speaker, or to decide which speaker made a particular point. This exercise will help you to focus on which speaker is making a point or expressing an opinion or attitude.

Listen again to the second part of Section 3 of the listening test and look at the statements below. As you listen, tick each point which Mark makes.

Stop the recording when you hear 'we'll get it done'.

		Mark	Anne
1	Fifty is the maximum number of questions allowed.	☐	☐
2	The number of questions in the questionnaire needs to be decided.	☐	☐
3	It is necessary to go up to the question limit.	☐	☐
4	The questions will be simple.	☐	☐
5	A mixture of question types would be a good idea.	☐	☐
6	It is best to ask people to tick boxes, rather than write things down.	☐	☐
7	People should be stopped and asked, both on the campus and on the street.	☐	☐
8	The questionnaires should be given out.	☐	☐
9	Ideas can be pooled.	☐	☐
10	Students are not as up to date as people think.	☐	☐
11	The focus of the questionnaire will be health and sport.	☐	☐
12	The assignment is not as bad as it seemed at first.	☐	☐

Now listen to the section again and this time decide which of the points Anne made.

Now check your answers to this exercise. When you have done so, decide if you wish to change any of the answers you gave in Section 3. Then check your answers to Section 3 of the test.

SECTION 4   QUESTIONS 31–40

Questions 31–35

In which year did the events below happen?

Tick (✔) the appropriate box.

	1810	1812	1814	1817	1818	1819	1821	1822	1824
Example Dickens was born		✔							
31 The first steam locomotive was built									
32 Waterloo Bridge was opened									
33 Dickens left London									
34 Several famous English novels were published									
35 Dickens moved back to London									

Questions 36–37

*Circle the correct answer **A–C**.*

36   In 1833

  A   *Chapman and Hall* was published.

  B   *The Pickwick Papers* was published.

  C   a steam boat crossed the Atlantic.

37   Which of the following took place in 1837?

  A   Queen Victoria became queen

  B   Dickens married Catherine Hogarth

  C   *Miscellany* was serialized

Questions 38–40

*Write **NO MORE THAN THREE WORDS** or **A NUMBER** for each answer.*

The serialization of *Nicholas Nickleby* began in **38** ....

The first postage stamp was introduced in **39** ....

and in the same year the first **40** .... was produced.

Stop the recording when you hear 'That's the end of Section 4'.
Now check your answers to Section 4 of the test.

ACADEMIC READING   60 minutes

READING PASSAGE 1

*You should spend about 20 minutes on **Questions 1–14** which are based on Reading Passage 1 below.*

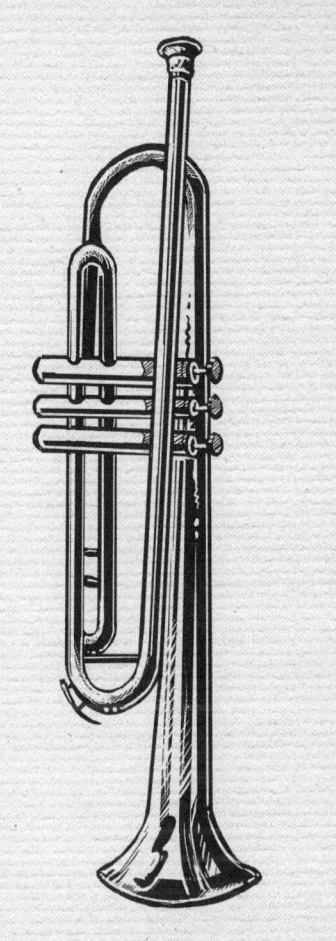

The instruments of the western orchestra are conventionally divided into four sections: woodwind, brass, percussion and strings. However, a much more comprehensive system for classifying musical instruments – ancient and modern, eastern and western, orchestral and folk – is also available. This alternative system, based on the work of Erich von Hornbostel and Curt Sachs, provides for the classification of musical instruments of all shapes and sizes according to how their sounds are produced. It begins by dividing instruments into four broad groups – aerophones, chordophones, idiophones and membranophones.

The first group, aerophones, contains any instrument that makes a sound when the air within or around it is made to vibrate. Further classification within the group is made according to how the air is set into vibration. Simplest are the so-called free aerophones (bull-roarers and buzzers), which consist of a flat disc twirled through the air on a string.

More typically, aerophones have a hollow tube or vessel body into which air is introduced by blowing. Sub-groups include instruments with a blow hole (most flutes) or a whistle mouthpiece (whistles and whistle flutes), in which the air vibrates after being blown against a sharp edge. In instruments with a cup mouthpiece, such as trumpets and horns, it is the action of the player's lips that causes the air to vibrate. Vibrations within a tube may also be produced by a reed taken into the musician's mouth. Such reeds may be single (clarinets) or double (oboes). Instruments classified as free reed aerophones, such as mouth organs and concertinas, have vibrating reeds within the body of the instrument. Organs and bagpipes are hybrid forms, each with pipes of different kinds.

The name chordophones is used for instruments with strings that produce a sound when caused to vibrate. Further classification is based on body shape and on how vibrations are induced. There are five basic types: bows, lyres, harps, lutes and zithers. The simplest musical bows have a single string attached to each end of a flexible stick; others have resonators to amplify the sound. Lyres, common in ancient times, have a four-sided frame consisting of a soundbox, two arms and a crossbar. The plucked strings run from the front of the soundbox to the crossbar. Harps are basically triangular in shape, with strings attached to a soundbox and the instrument's 'neck'.

Classified as lutes are all instruments with strings that run from the base of a resonating 'belly' up and along the full length of an attached neck. This sub-group is further divided into plucked lutes (round- or flat-backed), and bowed lutes (including folk fiddles and violins). The fifth type, zithers, have strings running the entire length of the body and are subdivided into simple zithers (stick, raft, tube or trough-shaped), long zithers (from the Far East), plucked zithers (such as the psaltery and harpsichord), and struck zithers (including the dulcimer and piano).

The third main group, idiophones, contains instruments made of naturally sonorous material, which are made to sound in various ways. They range in complexity from two sticks simply struck one against another, to tuned instruments like the orchestral glockenspiel. Idiophones are further classified according to the method of sound production into eight sub-groups: stamped, stamping, scraped, friction, shaken (bells and rattles), plucked (Jew's harps), concussion (when two sonorous parts are struck together, for example cymbals) and percussion (when a non-sonorous beater is used for striking). Percussion idiophones are further subdivided by shape into bars (metallophones, lithophones, xylophones), vessels (slit drums and steel drums), gongs and two types of bell (struck and clapper).

Hornbostel and Sachs termed their final broad group membranophones. In these instruments sound is produced by the vibration of a membrane or skin. Most drums fall into this category, being further classified by shape as frame, vessel and tubular drums, and by sounding method as friction drums. Tubular drums are further subdivided into long, footed, goblet, waisted, barrel, conical and cylindrical types. Much less important than drums are membranophones with an internal membrane vibrated by blowing, such as the kazoo.

The classification system of Hornbostel and Sachs, published in 1909, came before the burgeoning of electronic music in the second half of the twentieth century. The addition of a fifth group, to take in instruments that produce sound electronically (guitars, organs, synthesizers) would bring their system neatly up to date.

Questions 1–4

Choose ONE phrase from the list of phrases A–I below to complete each of the sentences 1–4 below. Write the appropriate letters in boxes 1–4 on your answer sheet.

1   Western orchestra instruments

2   In Hornbostel and Sachs' system, musical instruments

3   The classification of aerophones

4   Apart from the way sound is made, chordophones

A	are classified according to body shape.
B	are sometimes classified into four groups.
C	are usually classified into three groups.
D	are normally classified into four groups.
E	are classified according to sound production.
F	are classified according to volume of sound.
G	are classified according to sound quality.
H	is made according to how hot the air is.
I	is made according to how the air is made to vibrate.

Questions 5–12

*Using **NO MORE THAN THREE WORDS** from the passage for each space, complete the chart below.*

Types of chordophones i.e. 5...........................	Description
6...........................	Single strings attached to a single stick.
Harps	7........................... attached to a soundbox and the instrument's neck.
8...........................	with strings from the base of a resonating belly and along the length of an attached neck.
9...........................	10........................... with a soundbox, two arms and a crossbar
Zithers	are 11........................... into simple, long, plucked and 12........................... .

Questions 13–14

*Choose the appropriate letters **A–D** and write them in boxes 13–14 on your answer sheet.*

13   The writer states that

   A   electronic music fits neatly into the fourth group in the Hornbostel/Sachs classification system.

   B   the kazoo belongs to the idiophone group.

   C   electronic music is less important than other forms of music.

   D   a fifth group needs to be added to the Hornbostel/Sachs classification system.

14   Which of the titles below is the most suitable heading for the passage?

   A   Chordophones and idiophones

   B   Musical instruments reclassified

   C   A conventional classification

   D   The work of Erich von Hornbostel

Before you check your answers to Reading Passage 1, go on to pages 82–83.

FURTHER PRACTICE FOR READING PASSAGE 1

TEXT ORGANIZATION

Completion of tables and other diagrams may look complicated, but can in fact be a helpful way to present and organize information. The key is to understand the layout of the table and the organization of the text, decide what type of information is missing, and then extract the necessary detail from the reading passage.

Question 5

1   Does the text say what chordophones are?

   ....

2   Where does it say this?

   ....

Questions 6–12

1   Is the text in paragraphs 4 and 5 descriptive or argumentative?

   ....

2   Is the information in paragraphs 4 and 5 organized according to classification?

   ....

3   Put the words *zithers, chordophones, lyres, bows, lutes* and *harps* into the boxes below. Follow the order in the text.

		1................		
2..............	3..............	4..............	5..............	6..............

4   What is the relationship between the word in box 1 above and the words in boxes 2–6?

   ....

5   Are the words in boxes 2–6 also headings? If so, for what?

   ....

6   In the exam, the order of the table may be different to the text. How is the table organized on page 81?

   ....

7   The reading text as a whole is organized according to classification. Look at the last sentence of the first paragraph and put the five words that organize the text into the boxes below.

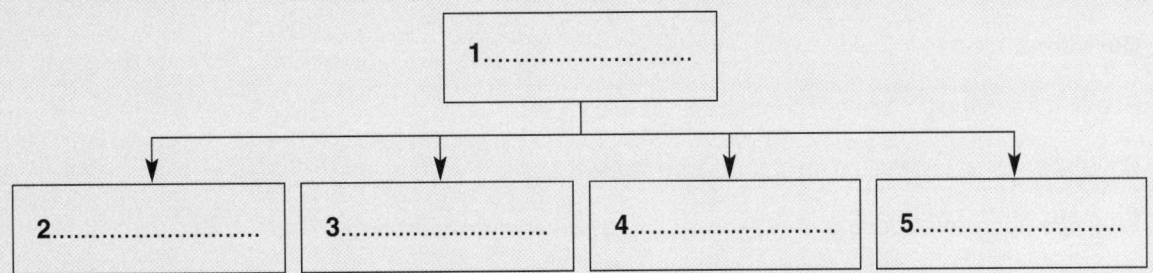

1..............................

2.................................   3.................................   4.................................   5.................................

8   Is the information on aerophones and idiophones organized according to classification?

....

Now check your answers to these exercises. When you have done so, decide whether you wish to change any of your answers to Reading Passage 1. Then check your answers to Reading Passage 1.

READING PASSAGE 2

*You should spend about 20 minutes on **Questions 15–28** which are based on Reading Passage 2 below.*

Questions 15–21

Reading Passage 2 has eight paragraphs labelled **A–H**.

Which paragraphs focus on the information below?

*Write the appropriate letters **A–H** in boxes 15–21 on your answer sheet.*

Note: You will not use all of the paragraphs.

15   Rapid development takes place on the west side of Southampton Water.

16   One factor influencing development on Waterside was the fact that there were few people.

17   The New Forest affects development on Waterside.

18   The site of an oil refinery is dictated by the land available.

19   Various limitations dictate the direction of expansion in Waterside.

20   Facilities like educational and sporting did not expand at the same rate as the housing provision.

21   Economic activity is the stimulus for suburban development.

Waterside: a study in suburban development

A   Since the 1950s there has been an increasing trend for extended housing and commercial expansion to take the form of rapid suburban rather than urban growth. There are several factors influencing the location and spread of such development, but an increase in economic activity is the trigger.

B   The area to the west of Southampton Water, now known as Waterside, exemplifies several factors impacting on the shape and nature of recent development. Up until the early 1950s this area, occupying a narrow strip of predominantly rural land approximately twenty kilometres long by five kilometres wide between Southampton Water and the New Forest, was relatively sparsely populated. There were a number of small villages, including Hythe, Fawley, Holbury, Dibden and Marchwood; communications were poor, and farming and associated industries were the main sources of employment.

C   The main town in the region, Southampton, was and still is one of the major UK ports. In the early part of the twentieth century, Southampton boomed as the growth in passenger numbers on transatlantic liners reached its peak. The main waterway leading to Southampton, Southampton Water, enjoys a long stretch of deep water channel suitable for large ocean-going vessels, and also benefits from an extended period of high tide because of its position in relation to the Isle of Wight. Existing settlement on the east side of the waterway made further expansion problematic, so a site was chosen on the west side to build a large oil refinery capable of handling the crude oil imported in the cargo holds of the enormous oil tankers then being built. The new oil refinery was built in the mid 1950s between Fawley and the coastal hamlet of Calshot.

D　The effects on the Waterside area were dramatic. Firstly, a major road was built linking the new Fawley refinery to the road network around Southampton. Also, a number of ancillary chemicals and plastics industries developed, dependent on by-products of the refining process. Work opportunities expanded and the population began to grow rapidly as workers and their families moved into the area. House-building took off.

E　The first areas to expand were around Fawley village, close to the refinery, and Hythe, the largest of the existing villages, with a ferry link to Southampton. However, although expansion in house-building was rapid, the development of a new commercial centre with a range of services and the provision of an expanded range of educational and health services or entertainment and sporting facilities did not initially take place. Partly, this was due to the proximity of Southampton, with its large range of facilities, now easily accessible through improved road links.

F　But there was another constraint on growth: the limited availability of land. Bordered on the east by Southampton Water, on the south by the sea, and limited to the north by the large village of Totton, almost a suburb of Southampton, there was only one direction expansion could go – westwards.

G　There were, however, limits here too. West of Southampton Water lies the New Forest, an area of ancient woodland and open heath, soon to be designated a National Park. Although it occupies a relatively small area, about 160 square kilometres, the New Forest is a complex and diverse ecosystem supporting a wide variety of plants and animals, many of which are found only in this area or are under threat in other parts of the country. There are stringent planning restrictions on all new building or construction of any kind. Moreover, these restrictions are supported by the local population living within the Forest, who are determined to preserve the unspoilt character of their villages and whose income is increasingly dependent on providing services for the growing tourist industry exploiting the Forest as a leisure resource. In short, development was channelled along a relatively narrow corridor parallel to Southampton Water. The space between existing villages was progressively filled with housing until they coalesced. Little farming land now exists between Dibden and Fawley; housing estates have taken almost all the land. The area around Marchwood, further from Fawley, remains more rural, but some development has taken place here too. Nor has any nucleated commercial centre emerged, though the existing village centres now have more shops, offices and a greater range of public facilities.

H　There is little room for further residential expansion in Waterside except in the area around Dibden Bay. Pressure for new housing development is now less, economic expansion has slowed considerably, and residents in the area are keen to preserve the bay area as a green open space with pleasant waterside views. But there is now a threat from another quarter. While passenger numbers using Southampton have declined, freight container traffic has continued to expand. The port area of Southampton has reached capacity. So the port authority are looking with speculative eyes at the one as yet undeveloped shoreline of Southampton Water with relatively easy access to deep water for large container ships – Dibden Bay.

Questions 22–25

*Using **NO MORE THAN FOUR WORDS** from the passage, answer the questions below.*

22 What were the main job providers in the area west of Southampton Water up until the 1950s?

....

23 What made building on the east of Southampton Waterway difficult?

....

24 How does the writer describe the consequences of the oil refinery on the coast?

....

25 What made it easier to reach Southampton from Waterside?

....

Questions 26–28

Do the following statements agree with the information in Reading Passage 2?

In boxes 26–28 on your answer sheet write

YES	*if the statement agrees with the information*
NO	*if the statement contradicts the information*
NOT GIVEN	*if there is no information about the statement*

> *Example*
>   Since the 1950s there has been an increasing trend for commercial expansion to take place in suburban areas.
>
> *Answer*
>   Yes

26 The New Forest has already been made into a National Park.

27 The people living in the New Forest are in favour of the limitations on development in the area.

28 Passengers going through Southampton are attracted by the charms of Dibden Bay.

Before you check your answers to Reading Passage 2, go on to pages 87–89.

FURTHER PRACTICE FOR READING PASSAGE 2

The questions below will help you to make sure that you have chosen the correct options for questions 15–21 on Reading Passage 2.

Paragraph A *Look at paragraph A and answer these questions.*

1 Does the paragraph tell you about suburban growth?

....

2 Is the paragraph organized around cause and effect?

....

3 A common organizational feature in writing is that of cause and effect. Which sentence contains the cause and which sentence contains the effect?

....

Paragraph B *Look at paragraph B and answer these questions.*

1 What is the area west of Southampton Water called?

....

2 Until the 1950s, was the area developed?

....

3 Until the 1950s, was the population large?

....

4 Does the paragraph focus on the factors impacting on the shape of recent development?

....

Paragraph C *Look at paragraph C and answer these questions.*

1 Is the paragraph mainly about Southampton?

....

2 Does the paragraph mainly focus on Southampton Water?

....

3   Is the paragraph mainly about the existing settlement on the east side?

....

4   Thinking of your answers for 1–3 above, what point is the author making?

....

Paragraph D *Look at paragraph D and answer these questions.*

1   How many effects does the paragraph describe?

....

2   Why were the effects described as dramatic?

....

3   In this paragraph are both cause and effect discussed?

....

Paragraph E *Look at paragraph E and answer these questions.*

1   Did the author write the paragraph in order to describe the expansion around Fawley village?

....

2   What is the significance of the word 'However' in the second sentence?

....

3   Is the paragraph about the range of facilities in Southampton?

....

4   What is the relationship between paragraphs D and E?

....

Paragraph F *Look at paragraph F and answer these questions.*

1   The first sentence of the paragraph mentions that 'there was another constraint on growth'. What was the previous constraint and where is it mentioned?

....

2   How many constraints are described in the paragraph?

....

3   What is the relationship between paragraphs F and G?

....

Paragraph G *Look at paragraph G and answer these questions.*

1   Did the author write the paragraph in order to describe the New Forest?

....

2   Is the structure of the paragraph basically that of cause and effect?

....

3   Is the New Forest another constraint on growth?

....

4   Find a sentence in the paragraph which contains a summary.

....

Paragraph H *Look at paragraph H and answer these questions.*

1   Why did the author write the paragraph?

....

2   Where does the paragraph divide?

....

3   Is pressure for housing development increasing?

....

4   Where is the pressure for development coming from?

....

Now check your answers to these exercises. When you have done so, decide whether you wish to change any of your answers to Reading Passage 2. Then check your answers to Reading Passage 2.

READING PASSAGE 3

*You should spend about 20 minutes on **Questions 29–40** which are based on Reading Passage 3 below.*

One finds oneself rebelling against a very controlled approach to education with its restrictions of centralization and, at the same time, against the liberal chaos that can at times prevail. There is a constant struggle between both camps of the educational divide, a struggle which invariably creates a jumbled mixture of educational provision. This is not to say that what is provided is totally unacceptable. Far from it.

In the educational world, picking and choosing from different theories, i.e. eclecticism, as is no doubt the case in many other fields, is frowned upon by the theoretical purist, irrespective of which of the two above camps they belong to. The pragmatists, i.e. practical classroom teachers, know that they have to jump from one teaching method to another, trying out new ones and discarding the old. But they frequently return again to tried and trusted techniques, sometimes with a fresh insight. Experienced teachers know that essentially there is not just one method, but that people learn in many different ways.

Some learners use a single method, but the most sophisticated employ an array of different techniques, instinctively or subconsciously, picking and even adapting any approach to suit their needs, while the not-so effective learners stick to a limited repertoire or even one method. The practicalities of the real world demand, however, that students and trainers in every field be eclectic.

Having a larger repertoire of strategies for learning, the sophisticated student advances at an exponential rate, as the different strategies he or she uses cross-fertilize and help each other. It is dangerous to exclude one particular technique in teaching or to follow one orthodoxy, as the one-size-fits-all principle does not, from a common sense point of view, work. It may deprive a weaker student of the only tool he or she may be able to use and deny the more effective learner an extra mechanism.

Take rote-learning, a much maligned learning process. There are certain aspects of any subject area, whether it be language or the arts or science, where a student is required to learn huge amounts of facts. These may be learnt by experience, but developing memory skills gives students an advantage in this area. Antipathy to certain methods like memory-based learning has condemned many students to a second-rate education, compounded by the fact that their teachers have been damaged by similar attitudes. It has been said that students are damned by the limitations of their teachers, just as the teachers themselves were damned.

This is not to say that rote-learning is the best approach to learning, yet it has its place as part of a wider programme. Where rote-learning proves inadequate is that it is not suitable for every learner. Not everyone is blessed with a good memory and learners should not be humiliated by not being able to learn things by heart. Other strategies need then be harnessed to compensate for this.

Electronic-learning

The search for ever more different novel learning styles goes on. Electronic-learning, or e-learning, is now very much the flavour of the month. The upside is that students may access the training whenever they want and they can learn at their own pace unhindered by fellow students. Again, whilst it has its place, e-learning lacks some essential ingredients, like the motivation of human contact in the classroom. Such training is, in fact, inherently flawed as it is impossible to devise an exhaustive programme to accommodate every individual. Learners have individual needs that may not be catered for by distance-learning delivered on the Internet. Frustrated by their lack of development, they will not develop to their full potential. One solution has been to build into any e-learning programme an element of human contact with on-line help via e-mail, but increasingly, as video-conferencing facilities become more advanced, designers are able to incorporate real-time video links. While this is a considerable advance, it still falls far short of the human contact that learning requires.

E-learning is here to stay, so what needs to be done is to give it a human face. Not, might I add, a computerized one, but a real one. Students should be able, if necessary, to access a tutor by telephone or, even better, face to face. Periodic tutorials could be built in to any programme. These can be individual, group and seminar or a mixture of all three.

Distance learning, such as e-learning, comes with an oft unheeded caveat. It is seen by the unwary as a cheap option and as a way of curbing costs. Set up on a wave of innovation and excitement, the initial wave of enthusiasm soon wanes. Few take on board the warning: any self-access material that needs to be developed requires huge amounts of input time. It has been estimated that, for every student hour, materials writers have to put in 70 hours of preparation. Those unfamiliar with the workings of materials production expect others to live through the consequences of their inexperience in this field. The wrong people, i.e. the materials producers, get the blame for any shortcomings: frequently, the quality and volume of material. There is one further point here that is worth mentioning. Once in place, the material requires constant updating and research: an added cost.

Questions 29–31

*Complete the following statements 29–31 with the best ending **A–G** below.*

*Write the appropriate letters **A–G** in boxes 29–31 on your answer sheet.*

29 There are, according to the writer, two educational camps: a centralized and

30 Unlike teachers, theoretical purists look down upon

31 The modern world dictates that students adopt

A	a flexible approach to teaching.
B	an over-controlled approach.
C	practical teachers.
D	various learning methods.
E	a controlled approach.
F	a liberal approach.
G	only a limited range of learning techniques.

Questions 32–36

Do the statements below agree with the views of the writer in Reading Passage 3?

In boxes 32–36 on your answer sheet write

> **YES**   *if the statement agrees with the views of the writer*
> **NO**   *if the statement contradicts the views of the writer*
> **NOT GIVEN**   *if it is impossible to say what the writer thinks about this*

32   Adopting one teaching technique rather than another depends on a whole range of issues which it is difficult for the writer to enumerate.

33   Rote-learning is an important learning strategy in all but a few subjects.

34   Rote-learning fails, because not every learner has a good memory.

35   Students are invariably humiliated by not being able to learn things by heart.

36   E-learning will not last long.

Questions 37–39

*According to the text, what are the **THREE** drawbacks of e-learning?*

*Choose three letters **A–G** and write them in boxes 37–39 on your answer sheet.*

A   The cheapness of learning by computer.

B   The cost of training teachers.

C   Not having enough trained personnel.

D   Not being able to cater for everyone.

E   The cost of keeping materials up to date.

F   Not having sufficient video-conferencing facilities.

G   Not having contact with people.

Question 40

*Choose the appropriate letter **A–D** and write the answer in box 40 on your answer sheet.*

Which of the following is a suitable title for Reading Passage 3?

A   Education in the modern world

B   Rote-learning and its drawbacks

C   Learning methods

D   A controlled approach to learning

Now check your answers to Reading Passage 3.

ACADEMIC WRITING   60 minutes

TASK 1

You should spend about 20 minutes on this task.

The table below shows the results of a survey of the average number of cars per hour using three suburban roads during working hours in a ten-year pollution monitoring programme. Traffic calming* was introduced in Harper Lane at the beginning of 1999.

Write a report for a university lecturer describing the data below.

*traffic calming = methods of slowing down traffic, e.g. by building raised areas across roads.

Write at least 150 words.

	1993	1994	1995	1996	1997	1998	1999	2000	2001	2002
Harper Lane	82	100	386	542	654	915	204	173	178	193
Great York Way	600	720	700	667	630	695	911	902	900	900
Long Lane	400	450	600	800	638	700	1000	1200	1400	1400

Before you write your answer to Task 1, go on to page 94.

FURTHER PRACTICE FOR TASK 1

1 *Look at the questions below and, ignoring the text on the right to begin with, study the instructions and table in Task 1 on page 93. These questions will help you to prepare the first paragraph of your answer.*

2 *Look at the introductory sentence below. Then match each question (1–7) with a section of the model answer (A–G) to continue the first paragraph.*

The table shows the average number of vehicles using three roads from 1993 to 2002.

1	Generally speaking, what happened in Harper Lane between 1993 and 1998?	A	increasing from an hourly rate of 600 vehicles to around 700.
2	What can you say specifically?	B	Great York Way saw barely any increase in traffic,
3	Was this increase ninefold or tenfold?	C	from just under an average of 100 vehicles per hour to over 900:
4	What can be said generally about Great York Way?	D	Between 1993 and 1998, the number of cars using Harper Lane climbed
5	What can be said specifically?	E	a ninefold increase.
6	What can be said generally about Long Lane?	F	by 75% in the same period, from 400 to 700 vehicles.
7	What can be said specifically about Long Lane?	G	The traffic travelling down Long Lane increased

3 *Now match each question (8–12) with a section of paragraph two of the model answer (H–L) below.*

8	What happened after the traffic calming was introduced in Harper Lane?	H	reaching around 900 vehicles in 1999 and hovering at this level till the year 2002.
9	What happened from then onwards?	I	and Long Lane witnessed a significant increase in vehicle numbers with the hourly average soaring to 1,400 in 2002.
10	What can you write about Long Lane?	J	After the traffic calming was introduced in Harper Lane at the beginning of 1999, the volume of traffic fell dramatically to an hourly average of 204 cars, considerably fewer than in 1998.
11	What can you write generally about Great York Way?		
12	What can you write specifically about Great York Way?	K	As regards Great York Way, numbers rose, but much less significantly,
		L	Thereafter, the number of cars stabilized at just below the 1999 level

4 *Now cover the right-hand column above with a piece of paper. Use the questions and the table on page 93 to write your own answer to Task 1, remembering to add a concluding sentence. When you have finished writing your own answer, look at the model and authentic student answers in the key on page 147 and compare what you have written.*

TASK 2

You should spend about 40 minutes on this task.

Write about the following topic:

Some people feel that certain workers like nurses, doctors and teachers are undervalued and should be paid more, especially when other people like film actors or company bosses are paid huge sums of money that are out of proportion to the importance of the work that they do.

- *How far do you agree?*
- *What criteria should be used to decide how much people are paid?*

Give reasons for your answer and include any relevant examples from your own knowledge or experience.

Write at least 250 words.

When you have written your answer to Task 2, go on to page 96.

FURTHER PRACTICE FOR TASK 2

1   *When you have finished writing your answer, use questions a–i below to help you check what you have written.*

a   Is the length of the essay appropriate?

....

b   Does the essay answer the question?

....

c   Does the essay contain any common mistakes?

....

d   Is there any repetition of words or phrases?

....

e   Is anything missing?

....

f   Are the paragraphs well linked together?

....

g   Does the essay contain a wide range of vocabulary and structures?

....

h   Is the overall organization of the essay good?

....

i   What is the function of each paragraph?

....

....

....

....

....

2   *Now look at the following model answer to Task 2 and answer the questions a–i on page 96.*

<u>How much people in certain jobs should be paid is a constant subject of debate with each profession extolling its own worth.</u> Nobody can deny that there are certain professionals like nurses, doctors and teachers who are essential to the fabric of society, and who should therefore be rewarded accordingly. However, <u>except in rare circumstances,</u> this is seldom the case <u>with professionals languishing at the bottom of the pay league</u>. When we look at the salaries and fees commanded by certain film stars and actresses and people who run large companies, this does not seem fair.

<u>However, there are certain things that need to be taken into consideration here</u>. First of all, not all film stars earn huge sums of money. In fact, at any one time in the UK, for example, roughly 80 per cent of actors are out of work and on top of that the number who are paid so-called 'telephone number fees' is even smaller. One must also remember that the career of many actors is very short and that therefore the money they earn has to be spread over many years. The same applies to company bosses, <u>but there are certain circumstances where this latter group does earn excessive salaries that quite often cannot be justified</u>.

Stating a set of criteria as to how much people should be paid is not easy. The idea of performance-related pay is very much in vogue at the moment <u>with employees having a basic salary which is topped up according to how much they achieve</u>. Rewarding people according to qualifications has long been used as a yardstick for paying people, but it is not a consistently good measure. Another is years of relevant experience, but there are many cases where a younger person can perform a task better than someone with lots of experience. Whatever criteria are used to assess salaries, an on-going cycle will develop. <u>As one group of professionals catches up with or overtakes another in salary terms, this will create pressure in other areas</u>. This considered, generally I feel that certain key professionals should have their salaries assessed by independent review bodies on an on-going basis so that they do not fall behind.

3   *Is it possible to remove the underlined parts of the text and still achieve a good score?*

....

Now check your answers to this exercise and compare your answer to Task 2 with the authentic student answer on page 148.

SPEAKING   11–14 minutes

PART 1 INTRODUCTION AND INTERVIEW (4–5 MINUTES)

In this part of the examination you will first be asked your name, and then you will be asked questions about yourself. Answer these possible questions:

1   Where do you come from?

2   Where do you live now?

3   Could you tell me something about your family?

3   What are your qualifications?

4   Are there any other qualifications you would like to gain?

5   How do you typically spend the weekend?

PART 2 INDIVIDUAL LONG TURN (3–4 MINUTES)

You will have to talk about the topic on the card for one to two minutes. You have one minute to think about what you are going to say and make some notes to help you if you wish.

Describe a celebration you remember.

You should say:

- what event was being celebrated
- the form the celebration took
- where the celebration took place
- who was there
- why it was enjoyable

and explain why it is memorable for you.

Now look at the Further Practice section on page 99.

PART 3 TWO-WAY DISCUSSION (4–5 MINUTES)

In this part of the exam, the examiner will discuss a topic with you. The topic is usually related in some way to the topic in Part 2, but the questions will be of a more abstract nature. Answer these possible questions:

1   What events in a person's life are most celebrated in your country?

2   What about the significance of gifts, are there particular presents that are given on particular occasions?

3   Celebrations such as weddings are often times when families gather together, what effect does this have on family relationships?

4   How is the way we celebrate events such as birthdays and religious days changing?

5   Do you think such changes are a good or a bad thing?

6   Which celebrations do you think will change the most in the next few years? How do you think they will change and why?

Now look at the Further Practice section on page 100.

FURTHER PRACTICE FOR SPEAKING

PART 2 INDIVIDUAL LONG TURN

In Part 2 of the speaking test you are asked to describe something. It is important to use a wide range of vocabulary. The following exercise will help you to focus on how you can improve your descriptions.

The sample answer below is acceptable without any extra words. Improve the description of the event by putting a suitable adjective or adverb in each space.

> I remember a **1** .... party I went to when I was a young girl. As far as I remember it was to celebrate the retirement of my **2** .... uncle. He had reached the age of 65 and the **3** .... company for which he had worked over the last 30 years organized a party in a **4** .... restaurant to mark his retirement. The celebration was attended by many people. A lot of them were his work colleagues, as well as family and friends. We all had a **5** .... meal and then there was dancing till late at night. The music was provided by a **6** .... band and everyone had a **7** .... wonderful time. It was a **8** .... enjoyable occasion as most people knew each other and were very relaxed. This celebration is memorable for me because I was a young girl and for once I was allowed to stay up late with the adults. I also remember that everyone was **9** .... happy, especially my uncle, who had a **10** .... smile on his face throughout the evening.

Does the description cover all of the points on the card?

Now check your answers to this exercise.

Now practise talking for one to two minutes about a celebration which you have attended. Try to use a variety of adverbs and adjectives.

PART 3 TWO-WAY DISCUSSION

The discussion in Part 3 of the speaking test is generally more abstract. Using examples and instances from your own knowledge or experience is a useful way to support the points you are making.

Below are some phrases which can be used to introduce a point relating to your own experience or knowledge.

To my knowledge, ...	My experience has been that ...
To the best of my knowledge, ...	I have found/noticed/realized (that) ...
As far as I know, ...	I remember when I was younger/was living in
In my experience, ...	London etc, ...

Think about a number of events that people celebrate, and specifically how they are celebrated in your culture. Describe each event, remembering to use the phrases in the box to give details from your own experience.

Events could include:

- *birthdays*
- *coming of age*
- *weddings*
- *funerals*
- *religious days*
- *special holidays*

TEST FOUR

LISTENING approximately 30 minutes

SECTION 1   QUESTIONS 1–10

Questions 1–6

*Circle the appropriate letters **A–C**.*

Example

The caller can book a car by pressing button number

(A) one.

B two.

C three.

---

1 The caller wants to

    A make changes to his car reservation.

    B complain about a car.

    C make a car reservation.

2 The booking reference is

    A ASFY15AG.

    B ACFY15AG.

    C ACFY50AG.

3 Mr Maxine originally booked the car for

    A Monday at 6 p.m.

    B Friday of next week.

    C this Friday.

4   Mr Maxine wants to change his booking to

      A   a larger manual car.

      B   five days.

      C   a smaller automatic.

5   Mr Maxine will have to pay an extra

      A   £165.

      B   £65.

      C   £15.

6   Mr Maxine rented a car

      A   five months ago.

      B   not long ago.

      C   several years ago.

Questions 7–10

*Use **NO MORE THAN TWO WORDS** or **A NUMBER** for each space below.*

7   The cost of the car hire changes ....

8   The manual estate is cheaper to hire than ....

9   Mr Maxine's credit card number is 3445 .... 7750.

10   Mr Maxine's address is .... Vale.

Stop the recording when you hear 'That's the end of Section 1'.
Before you check your answers to Section 1 of the test, go on to page 103.

FURTHER PRACTICE FOR LISTENING SECTION 1

MULTIPLE-CHOICE QUESTIONS

In listening comprehension exercises some of the points which appear in incorrect multiple-choice options may also be heard in the recording. It is important not to be distracted by details that appear in the questions in a different context to that in the recording.

The following exercise will help you to focus on choosing the correct multiple-choice options.

Listen again to Section 1 and choose the correct answer in each case.

Stop the recording when you hear 'I see'.

1   The caller has

    A   booked a car.

    B   picked up a car from Heathrow airport.

2   The booking reference contains the number

    A   50.

    B   15.

3   The original booking was for

    A   Monday evening.

    B   Friday evening.

4   Mr Maxine wants to

    A   change the size and type of hire car.

    B   reduce the hire period.

5   The difference in price includes extra costs for

    A   a longer hire period.

    B   a longer hire period and a different type of car.

6   The last time Mr Maxine rented a car was

    A   in the last few weeks.

    B   a long time ago.

Now check your answers to this exercise. When you have done so, listen again to Section 1 of the test and decide whether you wish to change any of the answers you gave. Then check your answers to Section 1 of the test.

SECTION 2 QUESTIONS 11–20

Questions 11–14

*Circle **FOUR** letters **A–F**.*

The Mystery Personality

A is a French speaker.

B plays for a well-known club.

C has got a famous wife.

D is very rich.

E has played for his national team.

F is a famous footballer.

Questions 15–19

*Use **NO MORE THAN TWO WORDS** or **A NUMBER** for each space below.*

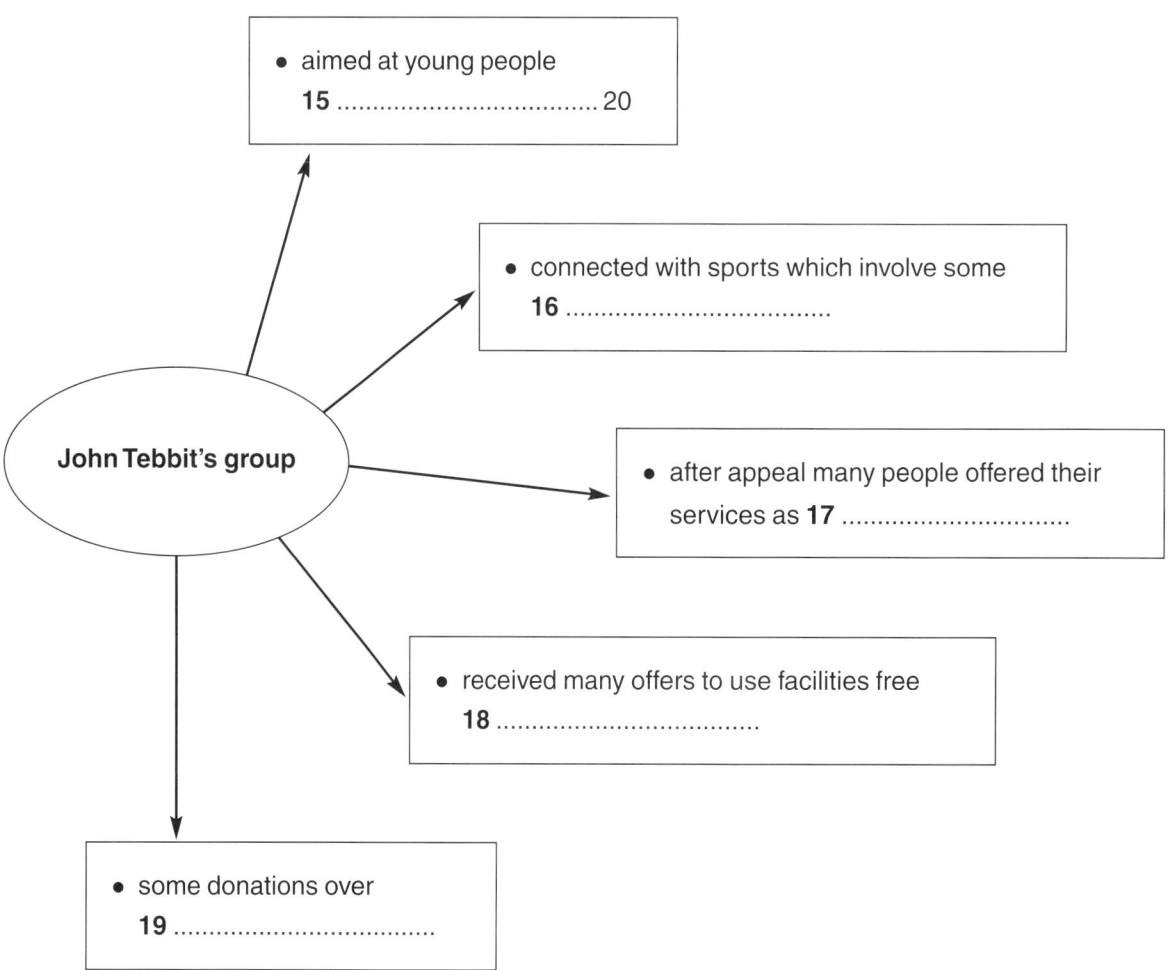

- aimed at young people
  15 20

- connected with sports which involve some
  16 ....

John Tebbit's group

- after appeal many people offered their
  services as **17** ....

- received many offers to use facilities free
  18 ....

- some donations over
  19 ....

Question 20

*Circle the appropriate letter **A–D**.*

20   Patrick

    A   had an accident three years ago.

    B   used to excel in archery.

    C   has been sponsored by one manufacturer.

    D   is not able to walk, but is very good at archery.

Stop the recording when you hear 'That's the end of Section 2'.
Now check your answers to Section 2 of the test.

SECTION 3   QUESTIONS 21–30

Questions 21–24

*Circle the appropriate letters **A–D**.*

21   Astrid says she is

    A   unhappy with Dr Adams.

    B   happy with Dr Adams.

    C   in the same tutorial group as Boris.

    D   in a different seminar group to Boris.

22   In the last lecture, Astrid took

    A   fewer notes than she thought she had.

    B   more notes than she thought she had.

    C   too many notes.

    D   not many notes.

23   Henry wants to copy Astrid's notes because

    A   Astrid's are neater than his.

    B   he missed the lecture.

    C   he was listening rather than writing.

    D   he didn't understand the lecture.

24   Astrid says Henry cannot copy her notes because

    A   her handwriting is difficult to read.

    B   they are too long.

    C   the photocopier is broken.

    D   he should have taken his own notes.

Questions 25–27

Write **NO MORE THAN FOUR WORDS** *for each answer.*

25 What is Astrid good at?

....

26 What was Adams' book about?

....

27 What do some intelligent people find it difficult to do?

....

Questions 28–30

Write **NO MORE THAN TWO WORDS** *for each answer.*

Henry

• useless at reading **28** ....

• brilliant at **29** .... and putting ideas

   down in the **30** ....

Stop the recording when you hear 'That's the end of Section 3'.
Before you check your answers to Section 3 of the test, go on to page 107.

FURTHER PRACTICE FOR LISTENING SECTION 3

In the listening test, you are sometimes required to give short answers to questions. A word limit will be given. In this type of question it is not necessary to give a full sentence as an answer. The type of information you need to listen for may be clear from the question.

Look again at questions 25–27 of the test and choose the best answer for each question below.

Question 25 The answer will be

a   a gerund or noun.

b   a time or date.

c   an adjective.

Question 26 The answer could be

a   a person.

b   a subject.

c   a book title.

Question 27 The answer will probably be

a   an object.

b   an activity.

c   an emotion.

In some questions you are required to complete sentences or notes. Again, a word limit will be given. As in questions 25–27, it is important to be clear about the type of information that is needed.

Look again at questions 28–30 of the test and decide on the type of information that is needed in each case. More than one answer may be correct in each case.

Question 28 The answer could be

a   something that is read, e.g. books, signs etc.

b   an adverb.

c   a percentage.

Question 29 The answer could be

a   a noun phrase or gerund.

b   a number or grade.

c   a place.

Question 30 The answer could be

a   a place.

b   a time.

c   a method.

Now check your answers to this exercise. When you have done so, listen to Section 3 again and decide whether you wish to change any of the answers you gave. Then check your answers to Section 3 of the test.

SECTION 4   QUESTIONS 31–40

Questions 31–36

Circle the correct letters A–D.

31   In a previous lecture, Dr North talked about

    A   the Marine Habitat Research Unit.

    B   humankind's relationship with sailing.

    C   humankind's relationship with the sea.

    D   the cost of fishing.

32   The focus of today's talk will be on

    A   problems the fishing industry faces worldwide.

    B   marine fish recipes.

    C   rare fish.

    D   European fishing problems.

33   A book list and relevant articles can be

    A   found only in the lecture room.

    B   found on the Marine Habitat Research Unit website.

    C   found in the lecture room and on the department website.

    D   taken by students for a small fee.

34   During the last century

    A   stocks of rare species have fallen dramatically.

    B   the world population has grown very fast.

    C   fishing has become less efficient but heavier.

    D   more people have decided to eat fish.

35   As well as over-fishing, which of the following is a reason for fishing stocks being on the point of collapse in the Pacific?

    A   Ocean ecology has changed.

    B   Fishing has spread to international waters.

    C   Fish has become cheaper.

    D   Oceans are more polluted.

36   In the UK

    A   fish used to be seen as a luxury.

    B   fish is not cheaper than meat.

    C   fish used to be seen as a cheap meal.

    D   food scares have driven people away from eating fish.

Questions 37–40

Use **NO MORE THAN THREE WORDS** for each space below.

Reasons why the number of fish is declining	A large **37**.............................. of catch nowadays is discarded.	**38**............................. and nets are to blame for the deaths of many fish.
Solutions to the problem	**39**............................. are not a complete solution.	Reducing the quantity of fish for each boat.
Example of disappearance of fish	Newfoundland, where **40**............................. disappeared.	

Stop the recording when you hear 'That's the end of Section 4'.
Now check your answers to Section 4 of the test.

ACADEMIC READING   60 minutes

READING PASSAGE 1

*You should spend about 20 minutes on **Questions 1–13** which are based on Reading Passage 1 below.*

Worms put new life into derelict site

Poisoned soil at an old steelworks is being cleansed by thousands of worms, writes Miml Chakraborty.

THOUSANDS of deep-burrowing earthworms are to help turn the long-derelict site of a steelworks into woodland and a renewable energy park.

As part of a pioneering low-cost plan to reclaim the site of the former Hallside steelworks at Cambuslang near Glasgow, worms are being used to accelerate the process of soil regeneration and to transform the land, over time, into an attractive and financially productive site.

Hallside's closure in 1979 put an end to more than 100 years of steel production. The surrounding land had become heavily compacted and was too contaminated with heavy metals such as chromium, cadmium and lead to support any kind of brick and mortar development.

The site's 30 hectares were left abandoned until 1990, when a rescue plan put together by local landscaping and earthmoving company, HL Banks, and the regional developer, Scottish Greenbelt, was approved by local authorities.

Now the site has been covered by a two-metre layer of partially treated sewage material which has been mixed with colliery waste. This will be converted into usable soil by about 21,000 *Lubricus terrestris* (garden lobworms) and *Aporrectodea longa* (black-headed worms) that have been let loose on the site.

The specially raised hermaphrodites, which are self-impregnating, will spend the next five to ten years chewing their way through the topping layer to create a soil structure able to sustain long-term plant growth. Without them, the process could take up to 60 years.

Researchers at Bell College of Technology in nearby Hamilton examined the use of earthworms in land regrading, and found that even in the hostile mixture of coal-tip waste and partially treated sewage, earthworms were able to speed up the process of soil recomposition.

They selected different varieties of deeper-burrowing earthworm species, whose bulk feeding and casting actions, as well as their ability to improve the mineral content of soil, would increase the rate of reformulation much faster than the natural processes.

Sean Ince, of Bell's department of biology, says: 'The idea is that earthworms will contribute in a cumulative way to further soil binding, and that they will aerate and add nitrogen to the soil covering the Hallside site.'

At the same time, Scottish Greenbelt has begun planting the area with 250,000 trees – including willow and alder – specially selected for their ability to grow on degraded land.

These will have the dual function of extracting contaminants from the soil through their root systems, and being harvested for wood burning or chipboard manufacture.

By using the cash raised from wood harvesting, David Craven, director of Scottish Greenbelt, says he expects Hallside to be self-financing.

'The first tranche of trees was planted in April and they are now over six feet tall, despite dry weather through the summer,' he says. 'The fields are being planted on a four-year rotation basis and will be used to help us meet our costs.'

Craven says the cost of land bio-remediation – the labour-intensive process of removing soil for chemical and bacterial cleansing – could have been more than £30m.

At Bell College, Ince says: 'There's a whole legacy of toxic soil contamination going back many years. There is physical degradation of the soil as well as contamination from metals, including lead, chromium and arsenic.'

Sampling of the soil at regular intervals over the next few years will give an indication of the level of contaminants. Within less than 20 years the land could be re-integrated into the community.

Hopes of a successful outcome at Hallside have paved the way for similar regeneration plans for the nearby Gartoosh steelworks and at Glengarnock in Ayrshire.

Questions 1–5

Choose the appropriate letters A–D and write them in boxes 1–5 on your answer sheet.

1   The Hallside site has been

    A   turned into a steelworks from a woodland and an energy park.

    B   in use as an energy park.

    C   disused for a long period of time.

    D   disused for a short period of time.

2   After more than one hundred years of steel production at Hallside,

    A   the land could not be used for anything.

    B   it was impossible to use the land to build on.

    C   the land could then be built on.

    D   the land could be used for any purpose.

3   The plan to reclaim Hallside was proposed by

    A   Scottish Greenbelt and the regional developer.

    B   local authorities.

    C   a local landscaping company and HL Banks.

    D   Scottish Greenbelt and HL Banks.

4   In the conversion of the soil at the Hallside site,

    A   two types of worms are being used.

    B   three types of worms are being used.

    C   many types of worms are being used.

    D   thousands of different types of worms are being used.

5   The soil regeneration at the Hallside site will take

    A   60 years.

    B   between 5 and 10 years.

    C   up to 60 years.

    D   less than five years.

Questions 6–9

*Choose **ONE OR TWO WORDS** from Reading Passage 1 for each answer. Write your answers in boxes 6–9 on your answer sheet.*

6   In research at Bell College, worms were used that quickened ....

7   The Bell researchers chose worms that would convert contaminated soil more rapidly than the

....

8   The soil at Hallside will be enriched by adding air and ....

9   Contaminants will be removed from the soil by ....

Questions 10–13

*Choose **ONE** phrase from the list of phrases **A–H** below to complete each of the following sentences 10–13. Write the appropriate letters in boxes 10–13 on your answer sheet.*

10   The Hallside site is expected to

11   Bio-remediation at Hallside could

12   Within 20 years, the land at Hallside could

13   Similar regeneration plans may

A	still be contaminated.
B	be in use again by the community.
C	work better elsewhere.
D	take place at other steelworks.
E	have cost millions of pounds.
F	have been labour intensive.
G	pay for itself.
H	cost more than bio-remediation.

Before you check your answers to Reading Passage 1, go on to page 113.

FURTHER PRACTICE FOR READING PASSAGE 1

Look at Reading Passage 1 and answer the questions below. This will help you to make sure that you have chosen the correct answers for questions 1–5 on Reading Passage 1.

Question 1 *Look at the first three paragraphs and answer the following questions.*

1   Has the steelworks been changed into an energy park yet?

....

2   Does derelict mean 'mis-used', 'disused' or 'useless'?

....

Question 2 *Look at paragraph three and answer the following questions.*

1   What is 'brick and mortar development'?

....

2   Is the land suitable for this type of development?

....

3   Does the writer mention any other purpose the land could be used for?

....

Question 3 *Look at paragraph four and answer the following questions.*

1   Who created the rescue plan?

....

2   Did the local authorities help?

....

Question 4 *Look at paragraph five and answer the following questions.*

1   The writer mentions garden lobworms. How many other types of worms does she refer to?

....

2   What does the number 21,000 refer to?

....

Question 5 *Look at paragraph six and answer the following questions.*

1   How long will it take to change the structure of the soil using the worms?

....

2   Will the worms take 60 years to change the soil structure?

....

Now check your answers to this exercise. When you have done so, decide whether you wish to change any of your answers to Reading Passage 1. Then check your answers to Reading Passage 1.

READING PASSAGE 2

*You should spend about 20 minutes on **Questions 14–28** which are based on Reading Passage 2 below.*

A I have recently planted a hedge. Living in a rural environment, I made the decision to plant only native species, including field maple, hawthorn, hazel, dog-rose and blackthorn. In time this will grow to form a dense hedge whose primary purpose is to form a windbreak, but which will also be attractive both to me and to wildlife. In the two years since planting, a number of hedgerow wild flowers, such as scabious and knapweed have already begun to colonize the spaces between the growing shrubs. Of course, if allowed to grow too freely, rank weeds and grasses will limit the growth of the hedge and need to be removed. This is done by hand, without the use of herbicides, in order to encourage bio-diversity.

B But it is not only native species that have found a foothold in the new growing environment. A number of garden plants of non-native origin have also established themselves. Some have come via wind-blown seeds, some through bird droppings, while others have arrived through human agency, stuck to the soles of boots or as dormant seeds embedded in garden compost. They include *Lychnis coronaria, Echinops ritro* and *Brunnera macrophylla*, all valued garden plants, but looking rather out of place in a natural setting. Such intruders are called 'garden escapes', and it isn't only my garden they are escaping from.

C In his recently published book, *Flora Britannica* (1998), Richard Mabey devotes a whole chapter to garden escapes. Many of these are relatively recent introductions, such as the Indian balsam which was first brought to Britain from the Himalayas in 1829, and *Fuchsia magellanica* which arrived about the same time. Both of these grow wild in Britain now; Indian balsam may be found along riversides and in damp places all over Britain, while *Fuchsia magellanica* is mostly confined to mild south-west England. *Buddleja davidii* was introduced from its native China in the 1890s and is now a ubiquitous shrubby weed of urban wasteland, derelict building sites or crumbling walls. Its dusky purple flowers are much frequented by butterflies and for this reason it is by no means an unwelcome interloper. Like the others it has succeeded by exploiting an ecological niche. No native British plant species has been able to colonize dry inhospitable urban landscapes to such advantage.

D Other vigorous aliens introduced as garden plants are now regarded as pernicious weeds. One such is Japanese knotweed, probably introduced into Victorian gardens in the 1840s. Its root system extends rapidly and it is able to regenerate from the smallest fragment of root. It forms dense thickets reaching 1.5 metres in height, under which no other plants can grow and little animal and insect life can be supported. It spread from London in the early 1900s and by the early 1960s was reported in every county of mainland Britain, reaching us even here in the remote Suffolk countryside. It is virtually ineradicable, and is now a serious pest in parts of south-west England. Another unwelcome intruder is giant hogweed, an undeniably handsome herbacious perennial, reaching up to four metres in height in damp meadows or open woodland, crowned with enormous umbels of white flowers. It, too, is invasive and its sap is also poisonous causing severe skin irritation and blistering, especially when activated by the ultra-violet rays of bright sunlight. Children are particularly at risk as the thick hollow stems and broad fan-like leaves lend themselves to a variety of games.

E This process is taking place all over the world. Plant species from one continent are introduced into the gardens of another, or as a food crop, or for hedging. They may then spread disastrously, taking advantage of suitable climatic and soil conditions, and of the fact that there may be no animal, insect or fungal predators in the new environment to keep them in check. The prickly pear, a spiny cactus originating in Central America, was introduced into Australia to control stock and keep out wild animals. It has now colonized vast areas of the Australian outback as both domestic animals and wild kangaroos and other herbivores find it virtually inedible. Prickly pear also grows now in parts of southern Arabia and is spreading rapidly. Even goats, which will eat almost anything of vegetable origin including cardboard boxes, find it difficult to deal with the dense spines of this cactus.

F   Many of the commercial food species now grown in Europe have also been imported from other continents, including potatoes, tomatoes and kiwi fruit. These do not readily spread across our landscapes, as they require constant human intervention in the form of irrigation, fertilizers, herbicides and insecticides. However, some agricultural crops can interbreed with wild species. Oilseed rape is one example. Plants are adaptable and have in their genes characteristics that enable them to survive and breed in a variety of conditions. Recently, with the development of genetically modified crops, some food plants have acquired new characteristics, such as resistance to drought, herbicides or insect attack. How long will it be before one of these genetic modifications transfers to a vigorous weed, escapes our global garden and goes on the rampage in the remaining wild habitats of the world?

Questions 14–18

Reading Passage 2 has six paragraphs labelled **A–F**.

*Choose the most suitable heading for paragraphs **A–E** from the list of headings below.*

*Write the appropriate numbers (**i–x**) in boxes 14–18 on your answer sheet. You may use each heading only once.*

One of the headings has been done for you as an example.

Note: There are more headings than paragraphs, so you will not use all of them.

List of Headings
i   Interbreeding between agricultural crops and wild species
ii   Examples from the *Flora Britannica*
iii   Planting a hedge
iv   The prickly pear – an unwelcome interloper
v   Keeping wild animals under control
vi   Plants escaping from the author's garden
vii   Bio-diversity
viii Virtually ineradicable
ix   Garden plants that have become weeds
x   Escaping plants

14   Paragraph **A**

15   Paragraph **B**

16   Paragraph **C**

17   Paragraph **D**

18   Paragraph **E**

Example	Paragraph **F**	Answer **i**

Questions 19–21

In which three paragraphs in Reading Passage 2 does the writer mention his own experience?

*Write the three appropriate letters **A–F** in boxes 19–21 on your answer sheet.*

Questions 22–27

Do the following statements agree with the information in Reading Passage 2?

In boxes 22–27 on your answer sheet write

YES   if the statement agrees with the information in the passage
NO   if the statement contradicts the information in the passage
NOT GIVEN   if there is no information about the statement in the passage

Example The writer lives in the country.	*Answer* Yes

22   The main purpose of the author's hedge is to form a windbreak.

23   The main route of escape for plants from gardens is by wind.

24   Indian balsam came from the Himalayas and grows only in the south-west of England.

25   The urban landscape in Britain has been changed dramatically by escaping garden plants.

26   The *Flora Britannica* (1998) by Richard Mabey is devoted to escaping garden plants.

27   Knotweed and hogweed are both invasive plants.

Question 28

*Choose the appropriate letter **A–D** and write it in box 28 on your answer sheet.*

28   Which one of the following is the most suitable heading for the passage?

A	Great escapes
B	Knotweed and hogweed
C	The *Flora Britannica*
D	Planting a hedge

Before you check your answers to Reading Passage 2, go on to page 117.

FURTHER PRACTICE FOR READING PASSAGE 2

MATCHING HEADINGS TO PARAGRAPHS

Be careful not to choose headings which refer to only part or one aspect of the paragraph. Some of the headings may contain words or phrases that appear in exactly the same form in the reading passage, so you may at first think they are correct. Remember that an example is usually given. Check carefully to see which paragraph has been done for you so that you do not waste valuable time searching for a heading that you do not need.

Look at the headings below for each paragraph in Reading Passage 2; some of the headings are suitable, but others are not. Select the suitable heading(s) in each case. More than one answer may be correct.

1   **Paragraph A**

   a   Plant species for hedges

   b   Creating a hedge

   c   Dealing with weeds in hedges

   d   Living in a rural environment

2   **Paragraph B**

   a   A new growing environment

   b   The growth of native species

   c   The spread of garden plants

   d   Garden escapes

3   **Paragraph C**

   a   Native British plant species

   b   Richard Mabey

   c   An ecological niche

   d   Plants from abroad

4   **Paragraph D**

   a   Pernicious weeds

   b   Pests in south-west England

   c   Unwelcome intruders

   d   Children at risk

5   **Paragraph E**

   a   Intercontinental spread of plants

   b   Worldwide process

   c   Lack of predators

   d   Virtually inedible

6   **Paragraph F**

   a   The need for human intervention

   b   Adaptability of plants

   c   Genetically modified crops

   d   Our global garden

Now check your answers to this exercise. When you have done so, decide whether you wish to change any of your answers to Reading Passage 2. Then check your answers to Reading Passage 2.

READING PASSAGE 3

*You should spend about 20 minutes on **Questions 29–40** which are based on Reading Passage 3 below.*

Day-dreaming
– an art or a waste of time?

Day-dreaming is generally viewed as an impractical, wasteful activity: one should be doing something useful, not just sitting or walking around with 'one's head in the clouds'. But rather than being of little worth, the capacity to fantasize is a priceless skill, a thoroughly useful tool, a tool for all seasons.

Day-dreaming is an essential ingredient in most, if not all, creative processes. In the pursuit of innovation and development, many organizations have been trying over recent years 'to capture the day-dreaming process' by formalizing and institutionalizing the process in creative seminars. Workshops where employees sit around 'brainstorming' and 'being creative' are now mushrooming. But do they work? To a certain extent they can, but not always. There are instances of outside consultants setting up brainstorming sessions for companies where the chairperson or director gives his or her ideas first. In doing so, they set the parameters as no one wants to contradict or overrule the boss. True brainstorming, like true day-dreaming, however, knows no boundaries, no hierarchies and no fears. The intention is not to disparage such activities, but they are too over-controlled and do not even mimic the environment needed to day-

dream and create. But they do show how the creative force, so frequently despised before, is creeping into the mainstream, even if in a contained manner. Very contained, in fact.

So where to begin? Day-dreaming or fantasizing is discouraged in children, so that by the time they are adults it has been completely removed. While one would not want to have all children sitting around in a kind of hypothyroidic haze of day-dreaming bliss, those most naturally inclined to it should be given space to dream and their ability nurtured. Creativity comes out of the unusual and needs space, in fact lots of space, to develop. Yet, life is based on mediocrity and so society demands that creative flair be knocked out of someone when they are young so that they can conform.

As adults, then, it is by and large more difficult to day-dream in general. The limitations have been set by others early on and by subtle reminders to keep people in place. Individuals in danger of deviating from the norm are kept in their place by a permanent flow of seemingly innocent comments designed to induce conformity ('I don't like that.' 'That won't work.') quite often delivered subconsciously. Fortunately, the die-hard day-dreamers/creators manage to struggle through.

Dreaming spots

For some of us, coffee shops, pubs or public places where people are moving around are ideal spots for day-dreaming. Or, indeed, somewhere where there is running water, by a river or stream. The constant movement seems to stimulate thought and ideas in a way that perhaps a library or the solitude of a study does not. It may not be possible to hone the finished text sitting around in a noisy café, but the challenge of holding together thoughts against adversity, as it were, is a great galvanizing force.

In the peace of one's home there are even more distractions, like the TV and the phone. People who are not familiar with the creative process may find it hard to accept that places like coffee bars are a source of stimulation. But why certain places and things motivate the creative individual and others do not is difficult to fathom.

Is day-dreaming an innate ability or something that can be taught? While I personally am prepared to accept that inheritance of ability does play a significant role in the process, I am more inclined to the idea that the environment, and perhaps chance, play a much greater role. It is said that genius is 10 per cent inspiration and 90 per cent perspiration. The coffee shop experience bears this out: a place of turmoil to engender the ideas and then back to the nest to flesh them out. The 90 per cent is a notional figure. If one looks at the work of the great inventors and artists past or present, one can see that more than 90 per cent of perspiration, as it were, went into the execution of their work.

Questions 29–35

Do the statements below reflect the opinion of the writer in Reading Passage 3?

In boxes 29–35 on your answer sheet write

YES	*if the statement reflects the writer's opinion*
NO	*if the statement contradicts the writer's opinion*
NOT GIVEN	*if it is impossible to say what the writer thinks about this*

Example	*Answer*
People think day-dreaming is a wasteful activity.	Yes

29 Day-dreaming is a worthless skill.

30 Organizations should be legally bound to institutionalize day-dreaming processes.

31 Brainstorming is totally effective.

32 In the day-dreaming process there are no limitations.

33 Most children should be given space to day-dream.

34 Young people need to have creative flair knocked out of them.

35 It is good that some day-dreamers survive the process of conformity.

Questions 36–40

Below is a summary of the second part of Reading Passage 3.

Using information from the passage, complete the summary.

*Choose **ONE WORD** from the passage to complete each space.*

Write your answers in boxes 36–40 on your answer sheet.

Busy places, where there is a lot of movement are **36**................ places to day-dream. Such environments help to produce thoughts and ideas. In fact, in one's **37**................ there are even more things to divert one's attention. It is not clear why the creative individual is **38**................ by certain places and things. The question is whether day-dreaming is **39**................ or can be learned. Inheritance, environment and chance all play a role in the creative process; supposedly only 10 per cent is due to **40**................ .

Now check your answers to Reading Passage 3.

ACADEMIC WRITING 60 minutes

TASK 1

You should spend about 20 minutes on this task.

The bar chart below shows the estimated sales nationally of silver goods* in '000s of units for two companies next year. The pie chart shows the projected market share of the two companies in silver goods at the end of next year.

Write a report for a university lecturer describing the information below.

Write at least 150 words.

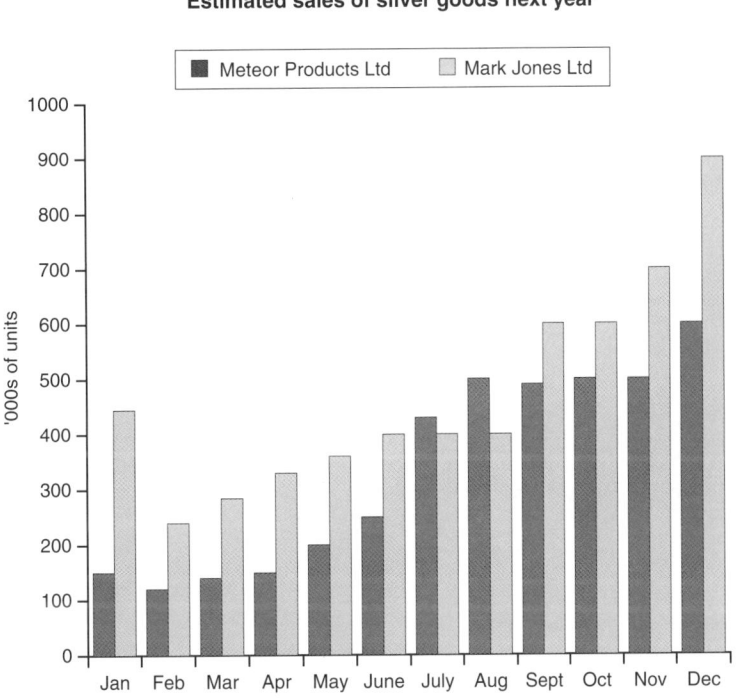

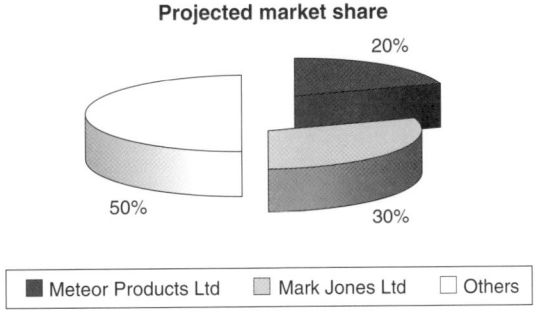

* *Note*: Silver goods refers to CD players, Walkmans etc.

Before you write your answer to Task 1, go on to pages 122–123.

FURTHER PRACTICE FOR TASK 1

1　*Look at the bar chart and pie chart in Task 1 on page 121 and answer the following questions.*

a　What does the bar chart show?

....

b　What is anticipated to happen to the purchase of silver goods from Meteor Products Ltd from January to August?

....

c　And what will happen from August until November?

....

d　What is the number of sales expected to be in December?

....

e　Meanwhile, what is estimated to happen to the sales of silver goods for Mark Jones Ltd from January to June?

....

f　What will happen in July and August?

....

g　And what will happen during the rest of the year?

....

h　What does the pie chart show?

....

i　What can be said about the overall sales trends for each company?

....

2   *Now look at the report outline below which has nine gaps in the text. Complete the outline using your notes from exercise 1. There is a vocabulary bank in the box below that you may want to use.*

The bar chart shows the **1** .... It is anticipated that purchases of silver goods at Meteor Products Ltd **2** ....

and **3** .... For December, sales are expected

4 ....

Meanwhile, **5** .... begin the year at around 450,000

units in January **6** .... For the next two months until

August **7** .... at this level, after which they are

expected **8** .... December.

The pie chart shows that at the end of next year, the anticipated market share for Meteor Products

Ltd and Mark Jones Ltd **9** ....

As can be seen from the chart, the overall sales trends for both companies are forecast to be

upwards.

Vocabulary bank

　　hit a peak　　increasing　　estimated　　approximately　　it is estimated　　falling to
　　　in the region of　　rise steadily　　respectively　　are forecast to　　remain until

---

3   *Compare your answers to exercise 2 with the model answer in the key on page 153.*

4   *Looking only at page 121, now write your own answer to Task 1. When you have finished, compare your answer with the authentic student answer on page 153.*

TASK 2

You should spend about 40 minutes on this task.

Write about the following topic:

> *Some people feel that the responsibility for providing education should be borne only by the government and that private education should be banned.*
>
> * *What are the main advantages of banning private education?*
> * *Are there any circumstances where private education should be allowed?*
> * *What is your own opinion on the matter?*

Give reasons for your answer and include any relevant examples from your own knowledge or experience.

Write at least 250 words.

When you have written your answer to Task 2, go on to page 125.

FURTHER PRACTICE FOR TASK 2

1   *When you have finished writing your answer to Task 2 on page 124 use questions a–f below to help you check what you have written.*

   a   Does your introduction reflect the two sides of the issue?

   ....

   b   Does your essay cover the three points in the essay question?

   ....

   c   Is the overall organization of the essay clear?

   ....

   d   In your answer to this essay question, is it necessary to mention the disadvantages of banning private education?

   ....

   e   Does your essay contain irrelevant information?

   ....

   f   Does the essay contain a wide range of vocabulary and structures? Can you avoid any repetition you may have included?

   ....

2   *Now compare your essay to the authentic student answer in the key on page 154.*

SPEAKING   11–14 minutes

PART 1 INTRODUCTION AND INTERVIEW (4–5 MINUTES)

In this part of the examination you will first be asked your name and then you will be asked questions about yourself. Answer these possible questions:

1   Where are you living at the moment?

2   What would you suggest a visitor to your home town should see or do?

3   What kind of things do you do in your free time?

4   How long have you been doing them?

5   What is it about them that you enjoy particularly?

PART 2 INDIVIDUAL LONG TURN (3–4 MINUTES)

You will have to talk about the topic on the card for one to two minutes. You have one minute to think about what you are going to say and make some notes to help you if you wish.

Describe a traditional meal in your country.

You should say:

• what the meal is
• how it is prepared
• when it is usually eaten
• what, if any, is the significance or importance of the meal

and explain whether you enjoy the traditional food of your country.

Now look at the Further Practice section on page 127.

PART 3 TWO-WAY DISCUSSION (4–5 MINUTES)

In this part of the exam, the examiner will discuss a topic with you. The topic is usually related in some way to the topic in Part 2, but the questions will be of a more abstract nature. Look at these possible questions:

1   What foods do you consider are good for you? Why?

2   What kind of things do people eat that are bad for them?

3   Why do you think people eat such things, if they are not good for them?

4   How do you think people's eating habits have changed over the years?

5   How could the eating habits of children be improved?

6   Why do you think people are concerned about chemicals and other additives in their food?

7   If you could, how would you change your own eating habits?

Now look at the Further Practice section on page 128.

FURTHER PRACTICE FOR SPEAKING

PART 2   INDIVIDUAL LONG TURN

Use the outline below to help you organize your answer. Complete the spaces with as much detail as you can and add examples from your own experience to make the description more interesting.

- There are many traditional meals eaten in my country, but the one I am going to describe is called

  ....

- It is made from (list ingredients) ....

  ....

- It is prepared by (give details of preparation) ....

  ....

  ....

- This traditional meal is often eaten (give details of particular dates, days or occasions and who

  usually eats the meal together) ....

  ....

- This meal is important because (give details of any cultural, religious or social significance of the

  meal) ....

  ....

- The traditional food of my country is (describe the cuisine of your country in general terms)

  .... ,

  and I enjoy/don't enjoy it because (give reasons) ....

  ....

Now, using your notes, talk on this topic for one to two minutes.

PART 3   TWO-WAY DISCUSSION

In Part 3, it is important to answer the questions as fully as possible using your own experience to support and expand your answers. Remember that the examiner is assessing you on your ability to use the language, not on the opinions you express.

1   *Match the questions in Part 3 on page 126 to the sample answers A–G given below.*

A   Such habits are dependent on a lot of things and change according to many factors. In recent times there has definitely been a move towards healthier eating, but I think that is because people have more choice than they did in the past.

B   There has been a lot more information in the media on this topic in recent years, whereas before people were, to a large extent, unaware of how their food was produced or what was put into it. Also, the dangers of certain pesticides and so on have been widely publicized.

C   The list is, unfortunately, very long: junk food in general, burgers, chips, takeaway meals, as well as lots of sweets and sugary drinks and biscuits, crisps and a whole range of other snacks and convenience foods.

D   There has to be a combined effort by both parents and schools; children need to understand the importance of healthy eating and this has to be made into an attractive alternative, rather than something which is boring and unappealing.

E   The most important thing is to have a balanced diet. Fresh fruit and vegetables are obviously good for you as they have a lot of vitamins and minerals in them, and it is also important to have some protein in your diet as well as carbohydrates and other elements.

F   If I had more spare time I would like to prepare and cook more fresh food for myself and my family, but in this day and age I, like so many others, am often tempted by the ease of convenience foods and meals.

G   People generally know what foods are best to avoid, but they don't really care. It only really becomes a problem if your entire diet is made up of foods which are considered unhealthy. I feel that it is fine to eat fast food and snacks, as long as you also have properly balanced meals.

Now check your answers to this exercise.

2   *Answer the questions in Part 3 on page 126 in your own words and using your own examples and experiences. You may want to refer to the list of phrases which are useful for introducing your own opinion on page 69 and your own experience on page 100.*

KEY AND EXPLANATION

TEST ONE

p8–15 LISTENING

FURTHER PRACTICE AND GUIDANCE (p14–15)

Gap-filling 1

1 A number, probably four digits, as the rest of the number is in this format.
2 A combination of letters and numbers.
3 A number, probably between 1 and 100. In Britain it is customary to have the house number before the street name, though this is not always the case in other countries.
4 A year.
5 A name. You may not be familiar with the term *maiden* (unmarried) *name*, but this should not mean you cannot do the task. It is clear that the answer will be a name of some kind.

Multiple-choice questions

6   How much/What has the caller paid?
7   What else is the caller worried about?
8   What has happened to the interest?
9   What is the caller's telephone number?
10 When will the operator ring the caller?

Key words

14 stopped smoking
15 people/not seeing him smoking
16 worst side effects
17 giving up smoking
18 easier/than
19 presenter/like to have
20 own/to success

Gap-filling 2

31 A noun or noun phrase, uncountable or plural. Here, *management* is part of a compound noun.
32 A noun or noun phrase, singular or plural.
33 A noun or noun phrase, probably abstract in this case.
34 An adjective or phrase to describe the type of tasks.
35 A gerund (*stop* is followed by either the gerund or the infinitive with 'to', with a difference in meaning), possibly with an adverb.
36 A gerund. Remember to look after the gap as well as before it. Here, *replying* tells you the missing word or phrase must be, or contain, a gerund.

37 An infinitive verb form, possibly qualified by an adverb.
38 A singular noun, beginning with a vowel sound (or there could be an adjective before the noun).
39 An imperative verb form.
40 A past participle as part of the passive form, possibly qualified by an adverb.

p8–9 LISTENING SECTION 1

Questions 1–5

1 3443
2 SE1 8PB
3 43
4 1963/'63
5 Moore

Questions 6–10

6 **B:** The caller says he has paid £500, but the computer says he has paid £300. The amount of 500 is mentioned, but the caller does not say he has paid it twice.

7 **C:** The payment to Pan Express is not one the caller recognizes. There is mention of a restaurant, but no mention of an overpayment, so B is not possible. As for A, no mention is made of paying too much.

8 **C:** The caller thinks that the interest has risen, but the operator corrects him. A is not correct as the interest rate went down, not up, in April. Since the interest went down, B is not possible.

9 **B:** The operator gets the number wrong, but the caller corrects her.

10 **C:** The operator says that she will call *straight back*, which means very soon. A is not mentioned and B is not correct as the caller says he will be *at home for the next two hours*.

p10 LISTENING SECTION 2

Questions 11–13

11 **B:** Mr Gold had breathing problems at the warm-up session. He couldn't touch his toes (C) because of his smoking (B), not because he hated smoking (A). Note that D is not mentioned.

12 **C:** He had to go across London to get cigarettes. There is no mention of his wanting to get exercise (A). Nor does Mr Gold say that he wanted to see

London at night (B); only that he drove across London at night to get cigarettes. Mr Gold says that he will give up anything to have cigarettes, even basic necessities (e.g. food), so D is not possible.

13 B: In the past he had found it difficult to give up smoking. Running (A), getting to sleep at night (C) and getting up early in the morning (D) are not mentioned.

Questions 14–20

14 1st July/July the first
15 cutting down
16 bad headaches
17 (exciting) adventure
18 expected
19 determination
20 road

p11–12 LISTENING SECTION 3

Questions 21–23

21 three/3 years
22 job
23 Wales

Questions 24–30

24 A: The tutor mentions the *faults* as the reason that Steve did not do better. The number of words is not a problem (C), and the book review is a separate piece of work (B). There is no mention of D.

25 C: The tutor said the book review *was the best we have ever had*, i.e. excellent. Therefore the answer cannot be D. The tutor does not say that the review was not as good as the project (B). In fact, the reverse is true. Steve is not criticized for writing too much (A).

26 C: The tutor says the end of the project *was a bit disappointing*.

27 B: The tutor suggests Frances should seriously consider doing an MPhil or a PhD. He does not suggest she shouldn't do an MPhil (A). There is no suggestion about C or D.

28 B: Frances' chances are as good as any other students', or even better than that. Therefore, A cannot be the answer. The grade depends on doing well in the exams. The tutor does not mention it in relation to the chances of getting a grant (C). The tutor does not compare her chances now with her chances in the past (D).

29 A: The tutor says it will be the *only First* for three years, i.e. the last one was three years ago.

30 C: Steve wants to earn some money so that he can afford to do the things he would like to do. Steve does not have to return to his job (D). He does not say he wants to stop studying (A).

p12–13 LISTENING SECTION 4

Questions 31–40

31 techniques and training
32 British economy
33 awareness
34 impossible
35 replying/responding
36 answering the telephone
37 respect
38 e-mail code
39 brainstorm
40 countered

p16–30 ACADEMIC READING

FURTHER PRACTICE AND GUIDANCE (p19–20)

Question 1

1 unjustified
2 **a**
3 gained/come to have
4 yes

Question 2

1 networking
2 No. It is talking generally.
3 ... *and not just in the business world*

Question 3

1 two
2 no
3 yes to both

Question 4

1 a networker
2 a non-networker or somebody who is not good at networking
3 no
4 yes

Question 5

1 it refers to inner/mental strength
2 no
3 no

p16–18 READING PASSAGE 1

Questions 1–5

1 **Yes:** The answer is in the first sentence of the first paragraph where the writer states that it is unjustified that networking is considered a modern concept. Note the use of the word 'idea' in the statement as a synonym for the word *concept*.

2 **No:** The answer is in the last sentence of the first paragraph. You need to read the end of the sentence, … *and not just in the business world*. Make sure you read around the information when you find it and not just jump to conclusions. The last part of the sentence in the text qualifies or restricts where the badge is worn.

3 **Yes:** The answer is in the first sentence of the second paragraph. The text does not mention a number, but it does indicate that there are two types of person. Note that students commonly want to put 'Not Given' as the answer here. However, the information as to the number is given.

4 **Yes:** The statement is a summary of the information in the first three sentences of paragraph two. Often, the exact words of the statement or sentence will not be found in the text itself, but the answer will be 'Yes' because the exact sentence is an accurate summary or paraphrase of the information in the text. Understanding meaning is being tested here. Just because the words or phrases in the statement are not in the text, it does not mean that the answer cannot be 'Yes'.

5 **Not Given:** The answer is in the third sentence of paragraph two: *The classic networker is someone who is strong enough within themselves to …*; the writer is talking about mental strength. The answer is 'Not Given' rather than 'No' because physical strength is not mentioned, so we do not know if the classic networker is physically strong or not. Note also that the writer does not mention anything about general health.

Questions 6–10

6 **brings success:** The answer is in the first sentence of the third paragraph. Note that you need to scan the text for possible synonyms of the words *new acquaintances* and *disadvantages*. Remember that you are looking for a negative word or idea to paraphrase the latter word. Note also that the answers to this section will follow the previous one in the text. This is usually the case, but is not always so.

7 **(very) insecure/jealous/envious:** The answer is in the second half of the third paragraph and the sentence is a paraphrase of the information in the passage. The technique here is to scan the passage for key words, *at work/manager*, or their synonyms. There is more than one answer here, which is also possible in the exam. You only need to give one answer.

8 **block:** The answer is at the end of the third paragraph. Note the use of the word *totally* in the question, so it is not possible to give *block completely* as the answer. As you scan the text for the answer, you need to look for synonyms of the words *manager/suppress/totally/career*. In this case, the first and last words are in the text.

9 **companies and enterprises:** The answer is in the first sentence of the fourth paragraph. The sentence to be completed is a paraphrase of this section of the passage. The words that help you to scan for the information are: *business/today/working together/grow*. In this case, you are looking for synonyms of the last three items.

10 **co-operation and contacts:** The answer is in the fourth sentence of the fourth paragraph. Note the key words for scanning: *Businesses that specialize* and *last*.

Questions 11–15

11 **(the) academic world:** The answer is in the first sentence of the fifth paragraph. Again, the approach here is to scan the text for the key words which will lead to the location of the answer. The words that help you scan here are *protected jealously* or their synonyms. The questions in this section follow on from those in the previous one, so the area of text to scan is decreasing. Note that, sometimes in the exam, the sections overlap.

12 **(the) stereotypical academic:** The answer is to be found in the third and fourth sentences of the fifth paragraph. The phrase *This sort of person … * at the beginning of the fourth sentence refers back to the sentence before, where the answer can be found. Your scan words are *type* (meaning sort) and *modern networker*.

13 **Cambridge/around Cambridge/Cambridge in England:** The answer is in the last sentence of the fifth paragraph; the word *Cambridge* would be enough, but a fuller answer is possible. The word *Europe* and the shortness of the text to scan makes this relatively simple.

14 *Homo sapiens:* The answer is in the last paragraph and is clear once the words *Neanderthals* and *replaced/superseded* have been located.

15 **culture:** The answer is at the end of the last paragraph and, in this case, the answer cannot be more than one word. Again, scanning the passage to locate the information already in the sentence to be completed is the key to finding the answer.

FURTHER PRACTICE AND GUIDANCE
(p25–26)

Question 16

1 yes
2 no
3 yes

Question 17

1 yes
2 yes
3 yes

Question 18

1 yes
2 yes
3 no

Question 19

1 yes
2 no
3 yes

Question 20

1 no
2 yes
3 no

Question 21

1 yes
2 yes
3 yes

Question 22

1 yes
2 no
3 no

p21–24 READING PASSAGE 2

Questions 16–22

16 **(iii):** The paragraph describes how reading became the mark of civilization. Heading (iv) is incorrect, because this heading describes only part of the content of the paragraph. It is the beginning of a development. It therefore does not cover the whole paragraph.

17 **(viii):** The answer is mainly in the first sentence, which is also the topic sentence for the paragraph. Heading (v) is incorrect as this is only one fact extracted from the paragraph. If you removed this piece of information would the paragraph remain intact?

18 **(xi):** The paragraph details how reading has developed into an economic force. Heading (ix) is incorrect as it is only one aspect of the paragraph.

19 **(vi):** This heading describes the cause and effect mentioned in the paragraph.

20 **(x):** This paragraph talks about the attitude that young people have to reading.

21 **(xii):** This short paragraph gives the writer's opinion of the decline in reading.

22 **(vii):** Note that the instructions state that any heading may be used more than once. This heading is suitable for this paragraph as well as paragraph H. Remember to read the instructions carefully or you could lose marks.

Questions 23–27

23 **Yes:** The answer is in paragraph B: *been satisfied with their achievements* paraphrases *rest on their laurels*. The scan words here are *European countries* and *overtake*, or the opposite, i.e. *fall behind*.

24 **Yes:** The statement is to be found at the end of paragraph C. Note the words *now no more just ..., but rather ..., fully-fledged ...* . The information is presented forcefully.

25 **Not Given:** The answer is at the end of paragraph D. We do not know to which degree the level of literacy in less developed nations/countries is higher; the quality is not mentioned. Ask yourself: is the literacy rate in less developed nations/countries higher ...? The answer is yes. Then ask yourself: is the literacy rate in less developed nations/countries considerably higher ...? The question cannot be answered.

26 **Yes:** The answer is in paragraphs G and H and is a summary of the text.

27 **No:** The opposite is true. The text states people should be encouraged to read them; the answer is at the end of paragraph G. It does not matter what people read. What is significant is the fact that they are reading.

p27–30 READING PASSAGE 3

Questions 28–32

28 **(v):** The answer is in the first line of the paragraph. The main distractor is heading (xi), but the paragraph is not about Wordsworth's sonnet, as the latter, although it occupies a substantial part of the paragraph, is subsidiary or supporting information; it is only an example to illustrate the form.

29 (vii): The paragraph is a clear description of the rhyme of the Petrarchan sonnet and an explanation of the reason for this. The distractor here is (i); the paragraph is essentially not about the octave developing the sestet, but about how both contribute to the rhyme scheme for the Petrarchan sonnet.

30 (iv): The paragraph is about an idea created by Howard (that was taken up and perfected by Shakespeare). Therefore heading (x) is not possible. The paragraph is not about the differences between the two.

31 (xiii): The paragraph is about variations in the structure of the sonnet form. One distractor here is (viii), but note that only Milton is mentioned as being unsatisfied. The other distractor is (ii), but this is only about a detail. The two headings are mentioned, but are not the theme of the paragraph. Can you remove the elements of (xiii) from the paragraph and still keep the meaning intact?

32 (vi): The question mark at the end of the heading is vital here. The paragraph describes Manley's variation, but in the last sentence raises the question of whether such a form can be classified as a sonnet. The distractor here is (xii) as only the last sentence of the paragraph focuses on this idea.

Questions 33–37

33 contemporaries: The answer is in the first sentence of the first paragraph. Note that the word needs to be taken from the passage, but it can be adapted (in this case, singular to plural) as the plural is needed to fit the structure of the sentence.

34 sonnet/little song: The answer is in the second sentence of the first paragraph. The word *it* at the beginning of this sentence refers back to the sentence before.

35 Petrarch: The answer is at the end of the first paragraph: ... *the latter* (or second of two previously mentioned things or people) *is regarded as the master of the form.*

36 fourteen lines/octave and sestet: The answer is at the beginning of the second paragraph: *consists of* is the same as *comprises.* The phrase *Complex poetic structure* would not fit here as the indefinite article would be needed, thus exceeding the word limit. For the alternative answer, see paragraph C, second sentence.

37 more: The answer is in paragraph C, where it is stated that the sestet is more varied.

Questions 38–40

38 C: The answer is in the second half of paragraph C. As with all questions of this type where a name is mentioned, the first step is to scan for the name in question. A is not true as Charles Gayley is not mentioned in connection with this. B is incorrect as this refers to the entire rhyme scheme and not just the octave (see the last sentence of the paragraph), and D is incorrect for this same reason.

39 C: The answer is in paragraph D: *Such a structure naturally allows greater flexibility for the author* (rather than the division into octave and sestet mentioned earlier, and referring back to the Petrarchan sonnet form). A is incorrect, as it is Howard who is mentioned as an indifferent poet, not his development. B is not correct because one sonnet form is not said to be more or less developed than the other. Alternative D is not right because the author says: *it would be hard, if not impossible, to enumerate the different ways in which it has been employed,* i.e. used in different ways, not counted in different ways.

40 D: The answer is in paragraphs E and F where the different sonnet forms of the poets are described. The key phrase is at the end of paragraph C: *a similar notion informs ... .* The other forms are noticeably different.

p31–35 ACADEMIC WRITING

FURTHER PRACTICE AND GUIDANCE (p32–34)

Task 1

1   a 8   b 5   c 8   d 7   e 3   f 2/5   g 6   h 6   i 4
   j 4   k 7   l 1

2   a   soared/rocketed
    b   plunged/fell back
    c   a sharp rise
    d   a steep fall
    e   dipped/fell back
    f   halved
    g   fluctuated
    h   dipped/fell back
    i   fell back/plunged
    j   a new peak

4   a   164 words – appropriate for the task
    b   yes
    c   There are no common errors in the text.

d Very little. The word *fluctuate* occurs in the second sentence of the first paragraph and again in the first sentence of the second paragraph. However, notice that a synonym, *fell erratically*, occurs in between. The word *hits* is repeated in the second paragraph, and could be replaced by the word *visits*.

e Yes. There is no conclusion. A general statement could be added at the end to summarize, for example: *Overall, although erratic, the trends for both sites are upwards.* This would increase the number of words to 174.

f The second paragraph is very well connected. Note the proper use of connecting devices such as *despite/whereas*. The writer also uses the *-ing* form of the verb to add specific information to a general statement: *… hitting a peak of over 120,000/reaching a total of over 150,000 hits on Day 11.*

g Yes, there is a very good range of vocabulary and structures. Again, look at the second paragraph: *fluctuated dramatically/Despite a drop* (as opposed to *dropped*)/*saw a huge increase/ peaked/showed a marked decline* etc. See also f above.

Note: This report is a possible band 8 because it is very well organized and connected. The range of vocabulary is good.

Task 1 Authentic Student Answer

> The graph shows people using new music places on the Internet in fifteen days period of time namely personal choice and trendy pop music.
>
> The overall trend shows fluctuation with slight Increased towards the end of the period.
>
> Starting with Music Choice websites; 40,000 poeple went on this new site on first-day. Half of them backed out the next day. In Contrast to this Pop Parade net sites were visited by 120,000 music lovers on day one which decreased slightly on the next day thereafter regaining the same fame on 3rd day.
>
> After 3rd day the enthusiasm for both music lines on Internet dropped slowly – reaching maximum fall of 40,000 on 7th day. Whereas Music choice gained popularity, slightly Improoving to get the original strength of 30 ,000 viewers on screen, but was getting still less visiters than their opponent Pop group i.e. 40,000 on day 7.

> In the biegining of the next week both gained remarkable recovery after a few fluctuations for 8th and 9th day having 40,000 and 50,000 visiters respectively, reaching to their peaks of one and a half thousand new viewers for Pop Parade on 11th day showing a contrast of very few people visiting Music choice for the same day. Thereafter Music choice gained popularity on 12th day for having more than 120,000 new visiters on web.
>
> In the end of the period Pop sites were visited by maximum viewers of 180,000 whereas sites located to Music choice were not explored by more than 80,000 explorers on the last day of the report.

Possible band 6. Well organized with some good linking devices and collocations (*gain popularity, remarkable recovery, decrease slightly*) and some valid comparison of the music sites. However, some sentences are long and confusing (paragraph 5), some collocations are inaccurate (*slight increased, reaching to their peaks*) and there is some repetition (*7th day, 3rd day, 11th day*). Some words are spelt incorrectly (*poeple, Improoving, visiters, biegining*).

Task 2 Authentic Student Answer

> The advanced 'Mind machines' so called 'the Computers' are no doubt the best products of latest technology. One cannot imagine the advancement of life and Sciences without these machines.
>
> But like other achievements; they have their own good and bad effects as seen with experience and passage of time. In my opinion they are good if used for educational and beneficial uses for health and living etc.
>
> Basically twentieth century had been famous for its latest Computer techniques and their application on our lives. Datas shown on Computers help us to assess how much education is conducted through this media. The assessment ways as well as examinations are improved. Moreover personal skills of reading and writing are far more improved through Computers.
>
> Moreover Science and technology progressed immensely with computers. Researchers like cloning and transplants are only possible with modern computerized skills.
>
> Good question comes to ones mind … where will this Computer would take us next?? Certainly no one knows! We might explore new plannets. May

> be we will buy houses on Moon, Mars or Jupitor. Or we might loose our own identity. One cannot forget the end of 2000 millennium when everybody was in chaos to think what will happen if the computers crash? The aeroplanes were going to crash and the trains would colloid. That show we are forced to think that one should not be dependent on these machine after all we are humans. We are here to command computers not them to order us.

Possible band 5. The candidate has attempted to organize some good arguments with valid examples and complex ideas. There is some relevant vocabulary (*cloning*) and synonyms avoid repetition (*bad effects* v *hindrance*, *good effects* v *help*). However, the arguments in paragraph 3 are not clear and the 'against' arguments are contained in the final paragraph, with no separate conclusion. There are frequent grammatical inaccuracies (*science and technology progressed, Researchers like cloning, where will this computer would take us, that show we*). This answer has also lost marks because it is too short (190 words).

FURTHER PRACTICE AND GUIDANCE (p37)

Part 1

Answers will depend on your particular circumstances.

Possible tenses:

A range of present tenses (including present perfect to express the duration of a situation or activity) when talking about your job, workplace, family, hobbies and interests; a range of past tenses when talking about your last holiday (including past perfect to refer to events before the holiday); a range of future forms when talking about ambitions (including *going to, will* and conditionals).

Useful items of vocabulary:

Job: company, position, duties, responsibilities, role, full-/part-time, to work shifts, to be promoted
Family: relationship, relatives, to take after someone, to get on well (with someone)
Hobbies: to take a hobby/interest up, to give a hobby/interest up, to be keen on something, to be into something
Last holiday: package holiday, to look forward to, to set off, sightseeing, resort
Ambitions: hope to be/do, wouldn't mind ...ing, intend to, would love to, plan to, dream of ...ing

TEST TWO

p38–46 LISTENING

p38–39 LISTENING SECTION 1

Questions 1–5

1 **B:** Hannah says she didn't think it was going to take her three weeks. From the conversation we can see that this is how long it actually took.

2 **C:** Hannah's father says it is because there are a lot of new students. Hannah agrees that is one reason, but then gives the number of new technology companies as the main reason, so B is incorrect. A and D are incorrect as neither of them are mentioned.

3 **C:** Hannah says *It isn't cheap for this area.* There is no mention of what she has paid before, so A and B are incorrect. D is the opposite of C.

4 **C:** Hannah says *I don't want to stay in this hotel any longer,* so A is not correct. The new accommodation is a flat and she wants to stop *living out of a suitcase,* so B and D are incorrect.

5 **B:** Hannah says her new flat is on the second floor. It is in a quiet street, so A is not correct; it has one double bedroom so C is incorrect. D is not right because the roof terrace is small.

Questions 6–10

6 **22b:** Hannah corrects her father.

7 **EX15:** Be careful: fif<u>teen</u> (stressed on the second syllable) can sound very like <u>fif</u>ty (stressed on the first syllable).

8 **evening after work:** Hannah hopes to travel to her parents' house on Friday evening after she has finished her work, and then bring her things down on Saturday afternoon.

9 **Saturday evening:** Hannah says she hopes to move her things on Saturday afternoon, but her father says he will pick the van up in the morning and then return it in the evening. He doesn't want to stay overnight.

10 **3/three hours:** He says the journey is *about three hours by road.* The phrase 'by road' cannot be used here as the word limit would be exceeded.

p39–40 LISTENING SECTION 2

Questions 11–14

H, F, E, B: The answers are given here in the order they occur in the recording.

Questions 15–18

15 **A:** Mr Funn, the Mayor, supports the planned developments.

16 **A:** The spokesman for the conservation group also supports the plans. Note that the speaker is surprised by this.

17 **B:** The local MP is against the plans.

18 **B:** The local shopkeeper is also against the proposals.

Questions 19–20

19 **A:** The phrase *the local college in Upton, which is not far from Tartlesbury* tells you that A is the best answer. B is not possible because it is the opposite of the answer. C is not mentioned in the recording and D is incorrect because it is a college that is mentioned and not a university.

20 **B:** The key phrase here is *this is the first time there has been a 100% success rate at the college,* so A is untrue, as is C. D is incorrect because there is no mention of this.

FURTHER PRACTICE AND GUIDANCE (p42)

1 e
2 f
3 g
4 d
5 b
6 a

p41 LISTENING SECTION 3

Questions 21–25

21 **five/5:** Dr Woodham points out that students have to write five essays over the year/course.
22 **50%/50 per cent:** The written exam accounts for 50% of the final marks and the course work, i.e. the essays, account for 50%.
23 **eighteen/18**
24 **fourteen/14**
25 **in the first tutorial**

Questions 26–30

26 relevant
27 (very) elegant
28 not possible / impossible
29 excellent
30 much better

FURTHER PRACTICE AND GUIDANCE (p45–46)

1 b
2 a
3 b
4 d
5 c

p43–44 LISTENING SECTION 4

Questions 31–35

31 B: Dr Butt mentions thirteen lectures: ten as part of the course in the morning and three extra evening lectures. Six to eight is the time of the evening lectures.

32 B: The average lunch break has decreased from 36 to 27 minutes, so C is incorrect; A is not correct as it is sick leave that is on the increase. As for D, the word *precise* is mentioned, but the 30 minutes is wrong.

33 A: The key phrase is: *the average figure is ten days per year, that's up by one day in 2002 compared to 2001.*

34 C: There will be a lecture on this topic *the week after next*, i.e. in about two weeks (a fortnight), so D is not right. A is incorrect because it is Professor Appleyard who will be giving the lecture. B does not make sense; the timing of the lecture can be seen on the calendar.

35 B: The key phrase is: *just below 50% of workers claim that they were taking less time off for holidays than they were entitled to.* This is a paraphrase of B. A is therefore clearly incorrect. C is not correct because this is the opinion of the speaker and not a fact, and D is not right because 'one third' refers to the number of days off sick and not the number of workers.

Questions 36–39

36 beyond their limits: The word order in the notes has been changed; in the recording it says *beyond their limits both physically and mentally*, but the notes to be completed require the phrases in a different order. This shows you that it is important to keep the information you hear in 'blocks' so that you can rearrange the component parts if required.

37 areas of industry: The information to complete the notes is in the right order this time. On the recording you hear: *productivity has gone up in many areas of industry.*

38 100: The number of vehicles per employee (or worker) is mentioned twice: for the year 2001 and 2002. You need to make sure you insert the information for the correct year.

39 collapsing: Here, 'thought' is a synonym for *considered*. It is important to listen out for possible synonyms to prepare you for the details you need to listen out for.

Question 40

B: Students who have opted to do the project have reduced the number of essays they have to do so C is incorrect. A is not right because the speaker says it would be interesting to do a survey of work life at the plant; it is not an option for the students to work there. D is not mentioned.

p47–62 ACADEMIC READING

FURTHER PRACTICE AND GUIDANCE (p52–54)

Question 9

1 in the last sentence of paragraph A
2 yes
3 no

Question 10

1 a
2 yes
3 two
4 a beneficial side and a destructive side

Question 11

1 yes
2 no
3 no – effects on the environment are mentioned
4 yes

Question 12

1 yes
2 no
3 yes – building river defences
4 planting trees

Question 13

1 to have no clean water
2 a third

Question 14

1 yes
2 it is probable that they will be under water
3 probable

Question 15

1 the last sentence
2 the first sentence of the paragraph: *Some might say ...*
3 no

p47–51 READING PASSAGE 1

Questions 1–8

1 **(x):** The paragraph deals with the dual relationship that humans have with nature. The answer is not heading (vi) as this is only part of the content of the paragraph.

2 **(i):** The paragraph talks about the fact that we have always had environmental changes.

3 **(v):** This paragraph deals with the idea that we feel better about our own property being destroyed by natural disasters if we are aware that it happens to others too. Heading (ix) is incorrect as this is only a detail in the paragraph.

4 **(iii):** The paragraph talks about the destruction caused by both rivers and seas.

5 **(viii):** The paragraph gives some solutions to the problem of flooding.

6 **(ii):** This heading is straightforward. Some headings may be relatively uncomplicated.

7 **(xiii):** The paragraph talks about various negative things that may happen in the future, not only flooding.

8 **(iv):** The paragraph talks about both of these aspects.

Questions 9–15

9 **D:** The answer is to be found in the last sentence of paragraph A. From the same sentence, it can be seen that A is incorrect – there is no mention of *gradually*. B is also incorrect because the opposite is stated. C is not correct because the text does not compare our need for water with anything else.

10 **A:** The answer is in paragraph B. The paragraph describes the two sides (positive and negative) of humankind's relationship with water. B is therefore incorrect. C is incorrect because the benefit is only one side of the relationship and D is not clearly mentioned.

11 **D:** The answer can be found at the end of paragraph C in the last sentence. A is not correct as it is not mentioned, nor is C; and B is wrong because the text says nothing about being left speechless.

12 **C:** The answer is to be found in paragraph F. A is not correct as it is not mentioned. B is the opposite of the correct answer and it adds the word *sea*, whereas the text is talking about rivers only at this point. D is incorrect as it is not mentioned.

13 **C:** The answer is in paragraph G. The text says that two-thirds of the world population will be without fresh water, so one-third will have it. Note that A is not possible because, like D, the numbers do not add up. As regards B, the majority will not have access.

14 **C:** The answer is in paragraph H. B and D are not correct as they are the opposite of C, and A cannot be correct if the islands are under water.

15 **B:** The answer can be found in the last paragraph of the passage, in the last two sentences. A is incorrect because, basically, it is the opposite. C is not stated and D is wrong because the end of the paragraph proves that the phrase at the beginning, *Some might say that this despondency is ill-founded*, is not actually true. The despondency is well-founded.

FURTHER PRACTICE AND GUIDANCE (p58)

Questions 16–22

1

16 **a:** Because of the use of the indefinite article here, it is clear that a singular noun is required.

17 **c:** Because of the plural noun after the space in this case, the required word must be an adjective. It is important to remember, however, that nouns can function as adjectives.

18 **a:** This time the position of the definite article before the blank indicates that a noun is needed and the verb form later in the sentence means that the noun must be singular.

19 **c/e:** This word must describe 'the government's lack of respect for the profession', so it has to be an adjective or possibly a gerund.

20 **e/c:** To complete the sentence a verb is probably needed, in this case in the present continuous form. Alternatively, an adjective would also fit here, but reference to the passage shows that it is the verb form which fits the sense of the summary.

21 **c:** Even if you do not know the meaning of the word 'series', the presence of the indefinite article before the blank tells you that it is a noun. Therefore, the missing word must be an adjective.

22 c: The verb form before the blank tells us that a descriptive word is required.

2 Paragraph 1

1 surprising
2 going into
3 attack
4 ten years

Paragraph 2

5 lack of respect

Paragraph 4

6 those who teach them
7 series
8 strain

p55–57 READING PASSAGE 2

Questions 16–22

16 shortage: In the passage the phrase is plural, *teacher shortages*, but in the summary the singular form is required.

17 teacher-training: This part of the summary is a clear paraphrase of part of paragraph one in the passage. Remember that hyphenated words count as one word.

18 profession: The answer is in paragraph one. Here, the noun phrase has been changed; *the teaching profession* in the passage needs to be changed to 'the profession of teaching' to fit in the summary.

19 obvious: Again, the noun phrase has been changed. At the start of paragraph two the passage refers to *the government's obvious contempt for the teaching profession*. The phrase has been changed in the summary, but the form of the word needed to fill the space need not be changed. (See 18 above.)

20 increasing: The answer is in paragraph three. The word needed to complete the space is the same as that in the passage, although in the passage it functions as an adjective and in the summary as a verb form.

21 recent: The answer is in paragraph four. Here, it is important to recognize the synonyms used in the summary for parts of the text: 'series' in the summary replaces *catalogue* in the text. Even if you do not know the meaning of certain words, you should be able to work out their meaning from their position in the relative sentences in the original text and the summary.

22 competent: The word needed to complete this space is the same as that in the text. The last sentence of paragraph four has been paraphrased, but the component parts of the sentence are largely used in the same form. It is the order of these parts that has been changed.

Questions 23–29

23 No: The opposite is true. In the first paragraph it states: *fewer students are entering teacher-training courses.*

24 No: The answer is to be found in the last sentence of the first paragraph. The writer is being ironic, given the facts stated in the paragraph there should be no surprise: *And the government wonders... .*

25 Not Given: The answer is in the third paragraph. This is what cynics would have us believe; the writer does not say if this is actually the case or not.

26 No: The answer is in the last sentence of the third paragraph: 'all teachers' is not the same as *most teachers*. Note that 'must' indicates deduction/conclusion and therefore opinion.

27 Yes: The answer is in the sixth paragraph. The problem here is the negatives. It is important to check that the text and the statement have the same meaning; in this case 'politicians are not as dangerous as educational theorists' has the same meaning as *politicians who know little about classroom practice or educational theorists who know even less, but are more dangerous.*

28 Yes: The answer is in the eighth paragraph. The statement is a paraphrase of the last sentence, but it is important to check carefully that there are no differences in questions of this kind; in this case the meaning is the same.

29 Not Given: There is no mention of this claim in the text.

Question 30

B: The theme throughout the passage is that the teaching profession does not get the respect it deserves from a number of sources. The other headings all refer to only specific sections of the text.

p59–62 READING PASSAGE 3

Questions 31–36

31 No: The answer is in the first paragraph and the key word *resounding* is in the first sentence; the writer says that the first piece of Hesse's work has a great effect on visitors.

32 Not Given: The first paragraph describes the first piece of art; order and the lack of order are described in this paragraph, but the writer does not say that understanding of order is necessary to understand the art.

33 Not Given: The second piece of art is described in the second paragraph, but there is no comparison made with the first piece described, so we do not know if the writer thinks the second piece of art is inferior to the first or not.

34 Not Given: The answer is in the second paragraph. The *irregular edges and non-conforming sides* are not design faults, but an aspect of the art. Whether or not the public is attracted to this aspect is not mentioned.

35 Yes: The answer is to be found in the fourth paragraph in the last sentence: *The associations seem to jump around in one's head, running between sensations of delight and pleasure, violence and discomfort.* i.e. the art arouses a range of emotions.

36 Not Given: In the passage the writer describes three pieces of Hesse's work as well as describing her work in general, but we are not told that the first, or any of the pieces, is preferred by the writer. There is no mention of a favourite piece.

Questions 37–40

37 A: The answer is in the first sentence of the sixth paragraph: *The visual language apparent in these artworks is unfamiliar, as is the artist.* B is therefore incorrect as the opposite is true; C is not mentioned and D applies to people who see her work, not to the artist herself.

38 B: The answer is in the last sentence of the sixth paragraph: *...her work was read in the context of its time where it has, until recently, been largely abandoned.* B is almost a paraphrase of this section of the text. There is no mention of A, and although the first part of C may be correct, there is no mention of the second part. D is not correct because in the eighth paragraph the opposite is implied.

39 D: The writer's opinion about how easy it is to define Hesse's work can be found in the final three paragraphs: her work is both *subtle* and *challenging*, so not easy to define.

40 A: The answer is in the penultimate paragraph: *We are now, more than ever, hungry for the cult of 'personality'... we seem in danger of focusing on the life of the artist, and not on the life of the art.* D is therefore wrong as the opposite is true; B is incorrect as 'personality' has a different meaning when with inverted commas to when it is without them; C is untrue as only one cult is mentioned.

p63–67 ACADEMIC WRITING

FURTHER PRACTICE AND GUIDANCE (p64–65)

Task 1

1 a Task 1 generally requires an objective answer. However, you may give some opinion if you wish.

b The factors can be divided into two groups, i.e. those where the two age groups more or less agree, and those where they noticeably differ in opinion. You could arrange your answer according to the age groups, but this might be more difficult.

c mentioned/cited/stated it as (*or that it was*) …

quoted/gave/rated/regarded/saw/viewed it as …

claimed (that) it was …

considered it to be …

You can also invert the sentence: *Regarding team spirit, it was mentioned as an important factor by 60% of those workers in each category.*

d Below are some useful variations. Can you think of others?

- Job security was much/far less important for the older group than the younger, at 20% as against/as opposed to/in contrast to 40% of those sampled.
- Job security was much/far more important for the younger group than the older, at 40% as against/as opposed to/in contrast to 20%.
- While/Whilst/Whereas job security stood at 20% for the older group, it was 40% for the younger.
- More workers in the younger of the two groups stated that job security was important, at 40%.
- Forty per cent of the younger group rated job security as being a factor affecting performance. By contrast, it was cited by twenty per cent of the older group.

- Only 20% of the older group gave job security as being a factor affecting performance, but it was mentioned by 20% of the older group.

2 a survey/out/namely
   b While/most/cited *or* given
   c given/importance/contrast/respectively
   d less/opposed
   e equally
   f regards
   g striking
   h differed
   i on
   j distinct

Task 1 Authentic Student Answer

The bar chart indicates a survey on two different age groups on the factors contributing to make their environment pleasant for working.

These factors are divided into external and internal factors. The internal factors are team spirit, competent boss, respect from colleagues and job satisfaction. The external factors are chance for personal development, job security, promotional prospects and money.

On the internal factors above 50% in both age group agreed that team spirit, competent boss and job satisfaction are essential to make their environment pleasant. Whereas on the external factors, there are contrasting results. On the chance for personal development and promotional aspects, 80% to 90% of the younger group were in favor while only less than 50% of the older group thought so. A similar pattern is also noted on job security. With regards to money, 69% to 70% on both age group said it is essential

In conclusion, the internal factors have similar responses from the two age groups while they had dissimilar responses on the external factors.

Possible band 7. The information contained in the bar chart has been described accurately and concisely and follows a clear progression. There is a clear introduction followed by effective comparisons between the age groups and a valid conclusion. Good formulaic phrases (*the bar chart indicates, these factors are divided*), although the candidate uses the same language to describe the factors in the bar chart and does not attempt to rephrase them in any way.

FURTHER PRACTICE AND GUIDANCE (p67)

Task 2

1 1A 2C 3C 4C 5B 6A

2 **Model answer for paragraphs 3–5**

Other people feel that keeping animals at home as pets is beneficial. They can help children and adults relate to animals and nature more. If children bond with animals early in life, they are more likely to treat them better when they become adults. My father, for example, was an only child, but in his early years he grew up with dogs, cats and birds as his companions. When he became an adult, he became a trainer for guide dogs for the blind. So having animals around can be beneficial to both humans and animals.

Moreover, pets can act as companions for people who would otherwise be living alone, and not just the elderly. There are at least two additional benefits here. Dogs need lots of exercise, which is beneficial for the health of the owner. Also, while out walking there is the opportunity to meet people, thus decreasing isolation and loneliness.

I do agree with the arguments put forward by the first group of people to a certain extent. However, I personally agree more with the second group of people. The world might be a better place if more people kept pets. As more and more people move away from direct contact with nature and see animals as a source of food or enjoyment, pets can provide a link between humans and nature.

Task 2 Authentic Student Answer

Despite integration of traditional (agricultural) form of families, people in many parts of the world, specially in the western countries are interested to keep an animal (normally dogs and cats, with themselves. Some people believe that pets are no longer so beneficial as the past but others argue that they are useful in many ways and should be kept in certain circumstances. I, generally, am inclined with the later group for many reasons.

The most important reason is that pet in some situations benefit people to a large extent. According to their abilities they could have great benefits. For example, a blind person who need some support, can benefit from a pet in term to go shopping, banking and other intercity journies. Another good example is using pets by the police and resue teams. In many situations where human senses are not able to diagnosis the problem, for instance smugling the drug, finding victims under rumbles of a ruins after an event a dog would be a better choice.

The second reason is that the mankind always need a friend and it is proven that dogs are good fried for the human. Living a pet with a family could have a positive impact on children besides olderly people. In some conditions pets have resued kids and other family members from a dangerous condition like firing and so on.

On the other hand, some people assert that keeping pets are belong to the past and should not be kept with families, because they are source for many disadvantages like diseases, some dangerouse states specially for newborn and toddlers and also their highly cost expenditure. For example they reffer to some special diseases like toxoplasmosis which can led to miscarriage near pregnant women, and also they bring some facts about being struk and even eaten kids by pets.

All in all I believe pets have more advantages and people can benefit them in special circumstances.

Possible band 7. There is a clear introduction and arguments for and against with some valid examples. However, the conclusion fails to develop 'the special circumstances' in which keeping pets is justified. Good range of vocabulary relevant to the task, but there are some lexical inaccuracies which affect meaning (*an agricultural form of families, a pet in term, rumbles of ruin*). There are also frequent grammatical errors which do not necessarily affect meaning (*interested to keep, pets are belong, living a pet with a family, diagnosis the problem, firing, source for many disadvantages, highly cost*) and some spelling mistakes (*resue, smuggling, fried* [friend], *dangerouse, reffer, struk*).

p68–69 SPEAKING

FURTHER PRACTICE AND GUIDANCE (p69)

Part 2

Suggested answers:
large – big, huge, sizeable, vast
hard – challenging, demanding, difficult, intensive, tiring, tough
because – since, as
nice – brilliant, fantastic, great, lovely, wonderful, gratifying, satisfying
good – beneficial, helpful, positive, valuable, worthwhile
very – enormously, extremely, highly, incredibly, wonderfully
pleased – grateful, relieved, thankful, thrilled
helping – aiding, assisting, supporting

TEST THREE

p70–78 LISTENING

p70–71 LISTENING SECTION 1

Questions 1–5

1 **have a coffee:** On the recording the actual words are *go and have a coffee*, but the word limit must be adhered to.
2 **September:** Note the correct spelling with a capital letter.
3 **on holiday:** 'holiday' alone is not acceptable.
4 **2/two weeks:** He is leaving tomorrow.
5 **Saturday:** Note the correct spelling with a capital letter.

Questions 6–10

6 **A:** The house is *the first on the right* after West Road crosses the bridge.

7 **B:** A is incorrect because the bridge does not belong to the house; C is not right because it is not mentioned.

8 **C**

9 **B:** The numbers are all very similar; it is particularly important to listen out for double numbers.

10 **A:** Each person has to give ten pounds as a contribution to refreshments and food, so B is incorrect. There will probably be a barbecue at the event, but the guests do not have to bring one, so C is not right.

FURTHER PRACTICE AND GUIDANCE (p73)

1 **main:** an adjective; on the recording the adverb is used.
2 **a list:** a noun; the article is needed as well. On the recording the passive is used.
3 **a/the choice:** a noun; the article is also needed. On the recording a verb form is used.
4 **be reviewed:** a passive form is needed. On the recording you hear a noun.
5 **lecture notes:** a noun or noun phrase. The noun phrase in the recording (*the notes you made at the lectures*) needs to be altered to fit in with the word limit.
6 **prepare:** verb; the *to* in the sentence tells you the verb must be in the infinitive form. On the recording you hear *do some preparation*, which is too long to fit the word limit of this exercise.
7 **count:** verb; here, the verb agrees with a plural subject (essays and project work). In the recording the subject is singular, so the verb form is different.

---

p71–72 LISTENING SECTION 2

Questions 11–13

11 **range:** The tutor says he may not be able to help in all situations, but he can refer students to *other support services in the university, ranging from...* . The gapped sentence needs the present simple form rather than the gerund as used in the listening script.

12 **a/the list:** To fit the grammar of the sentence the article is necessary here; without *a* or *the* the sentence would be grammatically incorrect.

13 **catch him:** The grammar of the gapped sentence requires a verb.

Questions 14–20

14 **B:** *...tutorials are voluntary; you are not obliged to attend.*

15 **C:** A lecture register started last year, but *this year, tutors are being asked to keep a register of tutorial attendance.*

16 **A:** In the exit questionnaire students said lateness of others was *the single most annoying thing.*

17 **B:** The lectures from *the week before*, i.e. the previous week, will be reviewed.

18 **A:** *Preparing a brief outline* is something that may be included, but *we are not expecting in-depth analysis at this stage.*

19 **C:** Note the negative in the stem of the question. A and B are included in continuous assessment grades.

20 **work and scores**

FURTHER PRACTICE AND GUIDANCE (p76)

1 Mark makes the following points: 4, 8, 11 and 12

2 Anne makes the following points: 1, 2, 5, 6, 9, and 10

Statements 3 and 7 are not made by either of the speakers.

---

p74–75 LISTENING SECTION 3

Questions 21–24

21 **D:** The students are talking about an assignment between 5,000 and 6,000 words in length. It is compared to four essays of 1,500 words, but this is not the answer in this case.

22 C: B is not correct because all three are mentioned; A is incorrect because the notes are about the assignment; and D is not right because these are for reference, not to be included as a whole.

23 B: The students have to prepare a questionnaire in draft form, A is the purpose for which the questionnaire is being created, i.e. to prepare data; C is untrue, and D is incorrect because collection of information will take place after the draft questionnaires are checked.

24 50/fifty (questions)

Questions 25–30

25 A: Anne says *I think we could have about 40 questions maximum,* but Mark does not show real agreement.

26 A: Anne suggests keeping the questions simple.

27 M

28 A

29 A: Anne suggests they *put together about 20 or 25 questions each... .*

30 M: Anne is going to type up her results and then they will play around with the layout on Mark's laptop.

p77–78 LISTENING SECTION 4

Questions 31–35

31	1814
32	1817
33	1817
34	1818
35	1822

Questions 36–37

36 C: A is not the right answer because Chapman and Hall are the publishers, and B is incorrect as *The Pickwick Papers* was suggested for publication (not published) in 1836.

37 A: Dickens married in 1836 so B is wrong, and C is not correct because *Oliver Twist* began serialization in the *Miscellany.*

Questions 38–40

38	1838
39	1840
40	bicycle

p79–92 ACADEMIC READING

FURTHER PRACTICE AND GUIDANCE (p82–83)

Question 5

1 yes
2 See the opening sentence of paragraph four. The table refers only to chordophones, so you need only look at paragraphs four and five.

Questions 6–12

1 descriptive
2 yes
3 In the diagram the order is 1) chordophones 2) bows 3) lyres 4) harps 5) lutes 6) zithers.
4 The word *chordophones* acts like a heading. Items 2–6 are subdivisions.
5 Yes. In turn, items 2–6 act as headings for the descriptions of the respective items.
6 The order is not the same. In the table the items are alphabetically arranged.
7 The main item is *instruments* which goes into box 1 with the words *aerophones, chordophones, idiophones* and *membranophones* in the subordinate boxes.
8 Yes, each with sub-groups.

p79–81 READING PASSAGE 1

Questions 1–4

1 D: The sentence is a paraphrase of the opening sentence of the reading passage.

2 E: The answer is in the penultimate sentence of the first paragraph: *according to how their sounds are produced.*

3 I: The answer is in the second sentence of the second paragraph.

4 A: The answer is in the second sentence of the fourth paragraph. It is easy to scan the text for the word *chordophones* as the word is unusual. It does not matter if you do not understand it. Note the last sentence of the first paragraph.

Questions 5–12

5 instruments with strings: The answer is in the first sentence of paragraph four.

6 bows: The third sentence in paragraph four lists the five groups into which chordophones are divided; *bows* is the first one that needs to be added to the table.

7 triangular with strings/with strings/strings: The answer is in the last sentence of paragraph four. Note that the items in the table are in alphabetical order, in the text they are not.

8 lutes: The first part of the fifth paragraph describes lutes.

9 lyres: The answer is in the fourth paragraph.

10 four-sided frame: To complete this space it is necessary to find the sentence in paragraph four that refers to lyres. Remember that hyphenated words count as one word.

11 subdivided: The answer is at the end of the fifth paragraph.

12 struck

Questions 13–14

13 D: The answer is in the last paragraph, in the last sentence. A is therefore incorrect because the classification system does not have a place for electronic music; B is incorrect because the kazoo is mentioned at the end of the penultimate paragraph, in the description of membranophones. C is incorrect as the importance of electronic music is not commented on by the writer.

14 B: The system described is an alternative system, as mentioned in the opening paragraph. C is therefore incorrect (see the opening sentence of the passage); A is not correct as these are only two of the many groups of instruments mentioned; and D is incorrect because Erich von Hornbostel did not work alone, but in partnership with Curt Sachs.

FURTHER PRACTICE AND GUIDANCE (p87–89)

Paragraph A

1 yes
2 yes
3 The first sentence contains the effect and the second sentence contains the cause.

Paragraph B

1 Waterside
2 no
3 no
4 no

Paragraph C

1 no
2 no
3 no
4 To show that development had to take place on the west side of Southampton Water. Note how the text builds up the picture and then the conclusion is drawn: ... *so a site was chosen* ... .

Paragraph D

1 five
2 There were lots of them and they were substantial.
3 No, only effects.

Paragraph E

1 no
2 It introduces the focus of this paragraph.
3 no
4 The developments that took place and those that failed to take place.

Paragraph F

1 The proximity of Southampton, with its large range of facilities – see paragraph E.
2 One main constraint, which is then explained.
3 The word *westwards* predicts what is going to be described in the next paragraph.

Paragraph G

1 no
2 yes
3 yes
4 The sentence beginning: *In short, ...*

Paragraph H

1 To show that the pressure on the land has moved from new housing development to the expansion in freight container traffic.
2 With the sentence: *But there is now a threat from another quarter.*
3 no
4 freight container traffic

p84–86 READING PASSAGE 2

Questions 15–21

15 D: Following the construction of the oil refinery (paragraph C) the effects on the Waterside area were dramatic and paragraph D describes how this area developed.

16 B: This paragraph focuses on Waterside prior to the 1950s. B could not be the answer for 15 above, as the situation before development is described in this paragraph, and not the development itself.

17 G: The focus of this paragraph is the effect that the New Forest had on the development that was taking place on Waterside.

18 C: The writer describes Southampton in detail, but the main focus of the paragraph is the siting of the oil refinery.

19 F: This paragraph, although short, describes several limitations which affected the expansion.

20 E: The main focus in this paragraph is the disproportionate development of facilities when compared to development of housing.

21 A: This paragraph describes suburban growth, but the main focus of the paragraph is the cause or trigger of this development, i.e. economic activity.

Questions 22–25

22 farming and associated industries: The answer is at the end of paragraph B; *sources of employment* in the passage has been paraphrased as 'job providers' in the question. It is important to be aware that the same words or phrases may not be in both the passage and the text, so as well as scanning for specific words it is important to look out for synonyms or related vocabulary items.

23 existing settlement: The answer can be found in paragraph C in the fourth sentence. It is important to distinguish between development to the east and to the west.

24 (they were) dramatic: Paragraph C describes the building of the refinery, and the answer can be found in the first sentence of paragraph D where the effects of the building are described. In this type of question short answers are required, so a complete grammatical phrase is not necessary. However, the words *they were* can be added and the answer still remains within the word limit.

25 improved road links/a major road: The first answer is in the last sentence of paragraph E. The second answer is at the beginning of paragraph D. So either answer is acceptable.

Questions 26–28

26 No: The answer is in the second sentence of paragraph G; the New Forest has not yet been made into a National Park, it is *soon to be designated* one.

27 Yes: The answer is in paragraph G: *Moreover these restrictions are supported by the local population living within the Forest.*

28 Not Given: The answer is to be found in paragraph H: it is stated that passenger numbers have declined and it is the residents that are *keen to preserve the bay area as a green open space with pleasant waterside views.* There is no mention in the passage of how passengers going through Southampton feel about Dibden Bay.

p90–92 READING PASSAGE 3

Questions 29–31

29 F: The answer is in the first paragraph.

30 A: The answer is in the second paragraph. The completed sentence summarizes the attitude of the purists.

31 D: The answer is in the third paragraph.

Questions 32–36

32 Not Given: There is no mention of this in the passage.

33 No: The answer is to be found in the fifth paragraph in the second sentence: *There are certain aspects of any subject area... .* The word *any* means 'all' in this case and is therefore not the same as 'all but a few'.

34 Yes: The answer is in paragraph six. The statement is a paraphrase of the following extract from the text: *Where rote-learning proves inadequate is that it is not suitable for every learner. Not everyone is blessed with a good memory ... .*

35 Not Given: The answer is at the end of the sixth paragraph in the penultimate sentence. The passage says that students should not be humiliated, but there is no mention of how often students are humiliated, i.e. invariably or not.

36 No: The answer is in the first sentence of paragraph eight.

Questions 37–39

The three drawbacks are: **D** and **G**, which are mentioned in the seventh paragraph, and **E**, which is mentioned in the last paragraph. The answers may be written in any order.

Question 40

C: Alternatives B and D are not correct because they refer to only part of the text. Alternative A is too general.

p93–97 ACADEMIC WRITING

FURTHER PRACTICE AND GUIDANCE (p94)

Task 1

2 **1** D **2** C **3** E **4** B **5** A **6** G **7** F

3 **8** J **9** L **10** I **11** K **12** H

> The table shows the average number of vehicles using three roads from 1993 to 2002.
>
> Between 1993 and 1998, the average number of cars using Harper Lane climbed from just under an average of 100 vehicles per hour to over 900: a ninefold increase. Great York Way saw barely any increase in traffic, increasing from an hourly rate of 600 vehicles to around 700. The traffic travelling down Long Lane increased by 75% in the same period, from 400 to 700 vehicles.
>
> After the traffic calming was introduced in Harper Lane at the beginning of 1999, the volume of traffic fell dramatically to an hourly average of 204 cars, considerably fewer than in 1998. Thereafter, the number of cars stabilized at just below the 1999 level and Long Lane witnessed a significant increase in vehicle numbers with the hourly average soaring to 1,400 in 2002. As regards Great York Way, numbers rose, but much less significantly, reaching around 900 vehicles in 1999 and hovering at this level till the year 2002.
>
> It can be seen from the data that traffic calming had the desired effect.

Task 1 Authentic Student Answer

> The data illustrates the conclusion of a study of the average number of cars passing on three different roads between 1993 and 2002. In general the trend was upword over the period.
>
> The most striking feature is that there was a dramatic increase in the number of cars passed on Long Lane from 1993 to 2001, during which the number increased from 400 cars in 1993 to 1400 cars in 2001.

> However, the number was fixed stable during the following year at 1400 cars.
>
> The evidence reveals that the number of cars on Harper Lane rose between 1993 and 1998. One year before the introduction of a traffic calming the number declined with a slight fluctuation.
>
> The facts show that the average number passed on Great York Way increased significantly from 1993 to 1999 the year in which traffic calming was introduced. There were 600 cars in 1993 and 911 cars in 1999. However, there was a very slight reduction in the number of cars during the following years.
>
> To sum up the introduction of traffic calming had a non significant impact on cars passing on roads Long Lane and Great York Way. In comparison there was a slight effect on the cars passing on Harper Lane.

Possible band 6. The candidate shows an ability to organize the answer and attempts to report notable trends displayed in the table. However, some ideas could be more clearly expressed. There is awareness of the language of movement, such as *trend, a dramatic increase, slight fluctuation, declined and increased significantly*. Although there are some lexical and grammatical errors (*upword, passed on, fixed stable, a traffic calming, non significant*), they do not generally affect meaning.

FURTHER PRACTICE AND GUIDANCE (p96–97)

Task 2

2 **a** yes, even though the answer is rather long
  b yes
  c no
  d no, there is very little repetition
  e no
  f yes – see use of *However, when, First of all, another is ..., This considered.*
  g yes – there is little if any repetition and a good range of vocabulary and structures has been used, e.g. *paid, rewarded, earn...money/salary/fee.*
  h yes
  i introduction; discussion about the salary of actors/company bosses; explaining the criteria for setting salaries; and conclusion.

3 You could remove any or all of the underlined text and still achieve a good score. If all were removed, the word count would fall to just over 250, which is acceptable.

Task 2 Authentic Student Answer

Whether workers like doctors and teachers are undervalued or not is a debatable issue. However, I believe that workers such as teachers and doctors should be paid more money for a countless reasons.

First of all, in my opinion, workers like teachers are more important for the society than actors. Therefore, they should be paid large sums of money to keep them educating people. Education is very essential for any society to progress and develop. Therefore teachers play an important role for performing this necessary aspect of development. Without teachers it will be impossible to know the basic levels of education, so teachers build students progress socially, intellectually and educationally. As a consequence of this teachers should valued according to this very essential role for the society.

Secondly, I personally believe that film actors/acleresses do not play the same role as doctors. Doctors protect people from spread of infections diseases which could damage not only the health of the general public, but also can deteriorate all aspects of our life. Without doctors, many well educated and productive people may be killed by diseases. Therefore, the doctors are very useful in health and progress which are necessary for any nation in the world wide. As a result of this position they should be paid some more money to keep the general public health and productive.

Thirdly, I largely disagree that film actors/acleresses are important. I think they do not take part in developing a nation's health and progress. Although they receive huge sums of money, they do not achieve any significant development for the society. I believe that their job is not as essential as health, economic progress and technological achievement. In contrast, progress and technological development as well as health of the nation depend mostly on teachers and health care works. Therefore, the latter should be more respected and paid to them the amount of money they deserve.

To sum up, I strongly be that works such as teachers and doctors are more important than film actors/acleresses. Therefore, the former should be considered more than the latter and paid to them accordingly to this essential role they do for the society.

Possible band 7. A full, well organized answer with well supported arguments. There is awareness of vocabulary and collocation relevant to the topic (*well educated, huge sums of money, general public*) and good use of linking devices (*first of all, secondly, thirdly, to sum up, therefore, as a consequence/result of this*) and language of opinion (*in my opinion, I personally believe, I largely disagree*). However there are frequent inappropriacies (*a countless reasons, infections diseases, students progress, acleresses, can deteriorate all aspects of our life, I strongly be that*).

p98–100 SPEAKING

FURTHER PRACTICE AND GUIDANCE (p99–100)

Part 2

These are suggested answers only. Many adjectives, adverbs and descriptive phrases can be used to make a description more interesting.

1 fantastic/retirement/wonderful
2 adored/dear/favourite
3 electronics/manufacturing/successful
4 well-known ('expensive/Italian' etc. would be possible with the indefinite article *an*)
5 delicious/enjoyable/fantastic/three-course
6 folk/jazz/local/talented/five-piece
7 most/really
8 highly/thoroughly/truly/very ('extremely' would be possible with the indefinite article *an*)
9 ecstatically/genuinely/so/really
10 beaming/big/huge/great

The description does cover all of the points on the card.

Part 3

Look at the topic card in Part 2 to help you organize your answer logically. A description could be organized as follows:

a the event that is celebrated
b the form the celebration takes
c the setting for the celebration
d the people who attend
e the procedure
f the reason for/meaning of the celebration.

Your own experience can be added at any time to explain, clarify or give an example of the point you are making.

TEST FOUR

p101–109 LISTENING

FURTHER PRACTICE AND GUIDANCE (p103)

1 **A:** The caller has booked a car to pick up from Heathrow airport. He has not yet picked up the car. Note that in the test question the word 'reservation' is used as a synonym of *booking* which is the word used in the recording.

2 **B:** There is often confusion between such numbers as 15 and 50. Note that '<u>fif**teen**</u>' is stressed on the second syllable, while '<u>**fif**ty</u>' is stressed on the first syllable.

3 **B:** The original booking was from *this Friday 6 p.m.* to next *Monday 6 p.m.*

4 **A:** The caller wants to change the type and size of car, and increase, rather than reduce, the hire period.

5 **B:** The extra amount the caller has to pay is made up of one figure (£15) which has been charged because it is a different car, and a second figure (not actually specified in the recording) charged for the extended hire period.

6 **A:** The caller rented a car *several weeks ago*, i.e. in the last few weeks.

p101–102 LISTENING SECTION 1

Questions 1–6

1 **A:** A synonym is used; the caller says he *booked* (past tense) a car and *I'd like to change the booking*.

2 **B**

3 **C:** A refers to the day and time that the caller, Mr Maxine, was originally going to return the car.

4 **B:** Mr Maxine wants to have a larger car, but he wants an automatic, not a manual car. So A and C are not correct.

5 **A:** The estate costs £15 per day extra, but this is only part of the full amount.

6 **B:** Mr Maxine says he rented a car *several weeks ago*.

Questions 7–10

7 **daily:** The *rates change daily according to the cars available*, but no more information can be included in the answer because of the word limit.

8 **the/an automatic:** The word *estate* cannot be added because of the word limit.

9 **9911 4425:** Note that the last four digits of the credit card number are present and do not need to be written in the gap. Repeating these numbers in your answers would be incorrect.

10 **40 Park:** Note that the final part of the address, *Vale*, is present and does not need to be written in the gap. Repeating this word would be incorrect.

p104–105 LISTENING SECTION 2

Questions 11–14

A, **B**, **E** and **F** in any order.

Note that *well-known* is a synonym for 'famous'. C is not correct as the speaker says the opposite. D is incorrect as the speaker doesn't mention money.

Questions 15–19

15 **up to:** In the recording you hear *young people up to the age of 20*, but the phrase needs to be shortened to fit the word limit of the question.

16 **expense:** In the recording you hear *some kind of expense*, but this must be shortened to keep to the word limit.

17 **volunteers:** Because of the word 'as' before the space, it would not be possible to put *free* as an answer.

18 **of charge:** The phrase is the same as in the recording.

19 **£5,000/5,000 pounds:** Numbers as well as words can be used to fill spaces in these types of exercises. However, in this case, *five thousand pounds* would exceed the word limit.

Question 20

D: Patrick *has been wheelchair-bound for the past five years*, but has also *excelled in archery*. A is incorrect because the accident happened five years ago; B is not correct because he excels in archery now; and C is incorrect because he is sponsored by more than one manufacturer.

FURTHER PRACTICE AND GUIDANCE (p107)

25 **a:** the answer will probably be an activity, something that Astrid is good at doing.

26 **a/b:** we would expect the answer to be a topic, so **b** is the most likely answer, although either could technically be possible. It is important to keep an open mind about what the answer could be.

27 **b:** the answer will be some kind of action, a verb in the infinitive form.

28 **a/b:** the answer could be either of these.

29 **a:** the students are discussing their abilities, so **a** is the most likely answer. Grammatically, **c** could also be possible, but is unlikely in this situation.

30 **a/b/c:** in this case each of the answers could be possible.

p105–106 LISTENING SECTION 3

Questions 21–24

21 **B:** C is untrue as Astrid is reporting what Boris said about that tutorial group, and D is not mentioned.

22 **B:** The key phrase is *I didn't think I had taken so many*; A is incorrect as it is the opposite of B; as is D; and C is not mentioned.

23 **C:** Henry says *I was that busy listening to what was being said that I didn't take many notes*; so B is untrue; A is incorrect because although true, it is not the reason that he wants to copy them; and D is not mentioned.

24 **A:** Astrid gives two reasons; the fact that Henry will not be able to read her handwriting and that she sometimes writes in Arabic. There is no mention of B; C is incorrect as Henry asks to photocopy the notes, but there is no mention of the machine being broken, and D is untrue because it is not a reason why Henry cannot copy them.

Questions 25–27

25 **detail**
26 **space and the individual:** Note the word limit in the instructions.
27 **read simple directions**

Questions 28–30

28 **maps**
29 **writing essays:** Note how the answers to questions 28 and 29 are close together.
30 **right order**

p108–109 LISTENING SECTION 4

Questions 31–36

31 **C:** The speaker says, *the lecture that I gave a fortnight ago on humankind's relationship with the sea ...*; A is incorrect because that is where the speaker is from; B and D are not mentioned.

32 **D:** The speaker says *In today's talk, I would like to focus on the current problems in the fishing industry in Europe ...*; A is therefore incorrect; C is not right as *scarcity of ... fish* (that there aren't enough fish) is not the same as 'rare fish' (unusual fish); and B is not mentioned.

33 **B:** A is not mentioned, so therefore C cannot be correct either. D is incorrect as there is no mention of a fee of any kind.

34 **B:** The speaker says: *During this time, the world population has grown at a phenomenal rate ...*; A is incorrect because the speaker does not mention rare fish. She talks about *heavily fished species*. C is not correct as it is only half true: fishing has become both more efficient and heavier; and D is not mentioned.

35 **A:** The reasons given are *a combination of over fishing and natural changes in ocean ecology*. Another reason is the change in people's eating patterns, but there is no mention of a drop in the price of fish, so C is incorrect; B is incorrect because it is the problem that has spread to international waters; and D is not mentioned as a contributory cause.

36 **B:** In the UK, *fish was once considered as food for the poor rather than the rich*; A is therefore incorrect as it is the opposite to this; C is not correct because *People have been turning to fish as a cheap and healthy alternative to meat ...*; and D is incorrect as people have been driven away from eating meat by food scares.

Questions 37–40

37 **proportion:** The speaker says *a sizeable proportion*. *Sizeable* is a synonym of 'large'.

38 **rubbish/(other) traps:** Note that, in the summary, the example (*discarded nets*) comes after the word *traps*, yet in the recording it is before.

39 **Fish farms:** The speaker says they *provide a partial solution*.

40 **cod stocks/(the) cod/(the) cod population:** The article can be included or left out here.

p110–120 ACADEMIC READING

FURTHER PRACTICE AND GUIDANCE (p113)

Question 1

1 no
2 disused

Question 2

1   buildings/structures with bricks
2   no
3   yes – used for an energy park/woodland

Question 3

1   HL Banks and Scottish Greenbelt
2   no – but they approved it

Question 4

1   1 (blackheaded worms)
2   the number of worms in total

Question 5

1   5–10 years
2   no

P110–112 READING PASSAGE 1

Questions 1–5

1   **C:** The answer is in the first paragraph: *long-derelict* (abandoned); A is incorrect as the plan is to do the opposite. B is incorrect, as the plan is to use it as an energy park in the future. D is incorrect as it is the opposite of the correct answer.

2   **B:** The third paragraph says: *… was too contaminated … to support any kind of brick and mortar development.* So C is not correct. As regards A, the text does not exclude everything; nor does it include everything as in D.

3   **D:** The answer is in the fourth paragraph. Note that Scottish Greenbelt is the regional developer, so A is not correct. B is incorrect because the local authorities approved the plan; they did not propose it. The local landscaping company and HL Banks are the same, so C is not possible.

4   **A:** Two types of worm are mentioned in paragraph five, '*Lubricus terrestris*' and '*Aporrectodea longa*'. The number 21,000 refers to the total number of worms used not the type, so C and D are wrong.

5   **B:** The answer is in the sixth paragraph. The regeneration will take up to 60 years if the worms are not used, so A and C are incorrect. D is incorrect, because it is between 5 and 10 years.

Questions 6–9

6   **soil recomposition/reformulation:** The answer is at the very end of paragraph seven. The word *reformulation* occurs in the eighth paragraph and is also correct.

7   **natural processes:** The answer is at the end of paragraph eight.

8   **nitrogen:** The answer is in the ninth paragraph.

9   **selected trees/tree roots/trees/special trees/planting trees/250,000 trees:** The answer is in the tenth paragraph.

Questions 10–13

10   **G:** Note that B is not correct here, as the beginning of the sentence indicates expectation and not possibility.

11   **E**

12   **B**

13   **D**

FURTHER PRACTICE AND GUIDANCE (p117)

Questions 14–18

In each case the incorrect answers are headings which may be used to describe a part, or one aspect, of the paragraph, but not all of it.

1   **b:** The other three headings relate to parts of the paragraphs. There are two ways here to check if the headings work: you can ask yourself if the meaning of the paragraph would remain if you removed the information in the heading. Another way is to ask yourself if all the information in the paragraph fits under the umbrella of the heading. Heading **b** is the only one which fits in both cases.

2   **c/d:** If you ask yourself the same questions as in 1 above, you can see that the other two headings do not work. Also, the paragraph is not about the environment (**a**) but about the plants growing in the environment. The paragraph does not just talk about native species.

3   **d:** The other three headings relate only to details. It is also important to remember not to restrict yourself to looking at just the first and last sentences.

4   **a/c:** The other two headings relate to details. Note first and last sentence here. 'Pernicious weeds' are mentioned in the opening sentence and 'children at risk' in the last sentence.

5   **a/b:** These two headings cover the global information in the paragraph and the other two relate to individual details. Note that you can fit

the two details in **c** and **d** under headings **a** and **b**, but not the other way round.

6 **b:** Heading **b** is the only one which covers all the detail in headings **a**, **c** and **d**.

p114–116 READING PASSAGE 2

Questions 14–18

14 **(iii):** The paragraph is about the writer's experience of planting a hedge; heading (vii) is not suitable here as it is only mentioned in the last sentence and in connection with one aspect of the paragraph.

15 **(x):** This paragraph concerns garden plants which have escaped; heading (vi) is incorrect as the last sentence of the paragraph states the opposite: *it isn't only my garden they are escaping from.*

16 **(ii):** The paragraph describes a number of examples from *Flora Britannica*.

17 **(ix):** The first sentence in this paragraph is the topic sentence and therefore gives the theme. Heading (viii) is not suitable because it describes only one aspect of one plant described in this paragraph, there are many other details given.

18 **(iv):** This whole paragraph is about one plant, i.e. the prickly pear. Heading (v) is not correct here as it relates to only a detail.

Questions 19–21

The following answers may be given in any order.
A: *I have recently planted a hedge... . I made the decision to... will be attractive both to me and to wildlife.*
B: *... and it isn't only my garden they are escaping from.*
D: *... reaching us even here in the remote Suffolk countryside.*

Questions 22–27

22 **Yes:** See the second sentence of paragraph A; 'main' is a synonym of *primary*.

23 **Not Given:** In paragraph B, the spread of a number of garden plants of non-native origin is described; 'by wind' is one of the methods by which they are spread, but we are not told whether this is the main method or not.

24 **No:** In paragraph C it does say that Indian balsam came to Britain from the Himalayas, but it says that it grows *all over Britain*. It is *Fuchsia magellanica* which is *mostly confined to the south-west of Britain.*

25 **Not Given:** The second part of paragraph C describes how *Buddleja davidii* has succeeded in growing well on urban wasteland, but we do not

know if it or other plants have 'dramatically changed' the urban landscape.

26 **No:** Mabey *devotes a whole chapter to garden escapes*; the whole book is not about escaping garden plants, only one chapter is on this topic.

27 **Yes:** The penultimate sentence of paragraph D begins: *It too is invasive ...*; Here, *it* refers to hogweed and *too* refers back to knotweed.

Question 28

A: The passage is about plants that have escaped and flourished elsewhere, so A is the most appropriate title. B is incorrect because it only refers to two of the species mentioned; C is not right because this is the name of a book mentioned in only one paragraph of the passage; and D is incorrect as this is the writer's experience, which he uses to lead into the main theme of the passage.

p118–120 READING PASSAGE 3

Questions 29–35

29 **No:** The writer says that day-dreaming is generally viewed as worthless, but in the second sentence of the first paragraph gives his opinion: *rather than being of little worth ... a thoroughly useful tool.*

30 **Not Given:** In the second sentence of paragraph two, the writer points out that organizations have been trying to formalize and institutionalize the day-dreaming process, but there is no information about whether or not the writer thinks organizations should have to do this by law.

31 **No:** The answer is in the second paragraph in the fifth sentence: *To a certain extent they can, but not always.*

32 **Yes:** The answer is again in the second paragraph, in the eighth sentence: *... true day-dreaming ... knows no boundaries ...'*, i.e. has no limitations.

33 **Not Given:** The answer is in paragraph three in the third sentence; the writer does not say how many children. But *those most naturally inclined to it should be given space to dream.* There is no indication of how many or what proportion of children that is.

34 **No:** This is not the opinion of the writer, but something that society demands; see the end of paragraph three.

35 **Yes:** The answer is to be found in the fourth paragraph in the last sentence. The key word here is *fortunately*, showing that the writer's opinion is that it is a good thing that some day-dreamers survive the process of conformity.

Questions 36–40

36 **ideal:** The answer is in the second line of the second part of the passage. The places listed are described as *ideal spots for day-dreaming*.

37 **home:** Note that only one word can be used.

38 **motivated/stimulated:** The answer is in the last sentence of the first paragraph. Here, the active form in the passage needs to be changed to the passive to fit the grammar of the summary.

39 **innate:** The answer is in the first sentence of the second paragraph. The direct question in the passage changes to an indirect question in the summary, but the form of the word required does not need to change in this case.

40 **inspiration:** In the second paragraph, the figure of 90% refers to perspiration and that of 10% to inspiration. Do not be distracted by figures, check carefully exactly what each one refers to.

p121–125 ACADEMIC WRITING

FURTHER PRACTICE AND GUIDANCE (p122–123)

Task 1

1/2 see model answer below

3 Model answer

> The bar chart shows the <u>estimated sales nationally of silver goods in '000s of units for two companies next year.</u>
>
> It is anticipated that purchases of silver goods at Meteor Products Ltd <u>will rise from 150,000 units in January to approximately 500,000 units in August, and will remain there until November.</u> For December, sales are expected <u>to be in the region of 600,000 units.</u>
>
> Meanwhile, <u>it is estimated that the sales of silver goods for Mark Jones Ltd will</u> begin the year at around 450,000 units in January, <u>falling to about 250,000, before increasing to around 400,000 in</u> June. For the next two months until August, <u>sales are forecast to remain steady</u> at this level, after which they are expected <u>to rise steadily to hit a peak of approximately 900,000 units in</u> December.
>
> The pie chart shows that, at the end of next year, the anticipated market share for Meteor Products Ltd and Mark Jones Ltd <u>is 20% and 30% respectively.</u>
>
> As can be seen from the chart, the overall sales trends for both companies are forecast to be upwards.

Task 1 Authentic Student Answer

> The bar chart shows the predicted sales of silver goods in '000s of units for two companies; Meteor Products Ltd and Mark Jones Ltd for next year.
>
> The most striking feature is that sales will increase for both companies. It is anticipated that sales of Mark Jones Ltd will start at 450,000 units in January decreasing by 200,000 units following month with a gradual recover over the subsequent four months reaching 400,000 units in June. Those of Mark Jones Ltd are predicted to be stable until August picking up to 600,000 units in September and October. Sales of Mark Jones will reach a pick of 900,000 in December. For those of Meteor Products Ltd is forecasted a gradual increase with the largest sale of 600,000 units in December. In the beginning of the next year those of Meteor Products Ltd will stand at 150,000 units falling back to 100,000 units in February, rising stadely to 250,000 in June. In subsequent months sales will reach 450,000 units increasing to 500,000 units in August, staying stable until November.
>
> Regarding the pie chart the sales of Mark Jones Ltd will share 30% of market whereas those of Meteor Products Ltd 20%. 50% of market is set to be shared by other companies.

Possible band 8. The candidate demonstrates the ability to organize the answer; there is clear progression from the introduction to the conclusion. The information contained in the bar chart and pie chart is clearly described. The candidate demonstrates a good command of phrases to describe notable trends and future trends (*The most striking feature is*, *It is anticipated that*, *predicted to be*). Although there are occasional grammatical and lexical errors (*following month* [the following month], *recover*[y], *pick* [peak], *is forecasted a gradual increase*, *stadely*), they do not generally affect meaning.

Task 2 Authentic Student Answer

> Whether or not education is a responsibility
> which only government should deal with and
> private education should be banned arouses
> some controversy. From my point of view, to some
> extent both types of education in a society are
> necessary.
>
> The primary argument for the opposite group is
> that education is not a privilage for only a group
> of people. From their view, private education can
> be a picture of discrimination between rich and
> poor families. For example, low income families
> who are not able to spend money for private
> schools would be deprived of studing and
> acadamic education. Also, people should be
> treated like each others and being affluent
> should not create any borders among pupils.
>
> On the other hand, looking at the issue from
> another aspect, highlights some points.
> Undoubtedly, the quality of education is quite
> wide in every society. Also, it is very likely that
> parents are not able to find a suitable school for
> their offspring. As a result they would be urged
> to look for private education. Furthermore, it is
> completely natural for parents to be concerned
> about their children's classmates, friends and
> even teachers. Therefore, they strive to select
> the best environment and best people for their
> children's education. It is a common belief among
> a most of the parents to that investing in a
> students education can be the ultimate project
> and the most they invest the best the result will
> be. Moreover, pointing to the first argument for
> the issue again, until the day when government
> provides a sound quality education in every parts
> of the country, the necessity of private
> education would be understandable.
>
> To conclude, in my opinion, in order to have a
> fruitful there should be a balance between both
> type of education.

Possible band 7. The candidate generally presents his/her ideas clearly and organizes the text. There is a wide range of relevant vocabulary and linking devices (*controversy, discrimination, low income families, deprived, affluent, offspring, classmates, strive to select, on the other hand, as a result, therefore, moreover, to conclude*) and some words and phrases used in the rubric have been rephrased (*deal with, primary argument*). There is awareness of set phrases but there are frequent inaccuracies in their use (*be a picture of discrimination, create any borders among pupils, a sound quality education, to have a fruitful*).

p126–128 SPEAKING

FURTHER PRACTICE AND GUIDANCE (p127–128)

Part 3

1 1 E
   2 C
   3 G
   4 A
   5 D
   6 B
   7 F

LISTENING SCRIPTS

TEST ONE   SECTION 1

Questions 1–5

CALL CENTRE OPERATOR: Platinum Card Service. Rebecca speaking. How may I help you?

CALLER: I've got a few problems with my credit card account.

OPERATOR: Okay. What is your credit card number?

CALLER: Let's see. It's here somewhere. Ah, here it is.

[Repeat]

OPERATOR: Can I just take the card number, please?

CALLER: Yes, it's 6992.

OPERATOR: 6992.

CALLER: 3443.

OPERATOR: 3443.

CALLER: 1147.

OPERATOR: 1147.

CALLER: 8921.

OPERATOR: 8921. Right. Can I just check that? Ahm, 6992 3443 1147 8921.

CALLER: That's it.

OPERATOR: And your name?

CALLER: Carlos da Silva.

OPERATOR: I just need to check a few details for identification and security, if you'll bear with me.

CALLER: That's okay.

OPERATOR: And what's your postcode?

CALLER: SE1 8PB.

OPERATOR: SE1 8PB.

CALLER: That's it.

OPERATOR: Vauxhall Close, London?

CALLER: Yes. That's right.

OPERATOR: And the house number?

CALLER: Ahm, 43.

OPERATOR: And can you give me your date of birth?

CALLER: 13th of the 7th, '63.

OPERATOR: And one further check, if I may? Can you give me your mother's maiden name?

CALLER: Yes. It's Moore.

OPERATOR: Is that M. O. O. R. E.?

CALLER: Yes. That's it.

Questions 6–10

CALLER: Yes. Now, can we get on with this?

OPERATOR: Yes, Sir. Certainly. I'm sure you'll appreciate that all these checks are necessary for security reasons. So what exactly is the problem?

CALLER: Problems.

OPERATOR: Okay.

CALLER: Well, first, mmm, your computer seems to have gone mad. I sent you £500 and on the statement for the account it shows that I only paid £300.

OPERATOR: Yes. The account does only show £300 was paid …

CALLER: Well, I paid the £500 in at the bank and I have my receipt. And my bank statement shows that £500 has been taken from my account.

OPERATOR: Oh. I see. What I'll do is check with the bank and see what they say.

CALLER: Okay.

OPERATOR: You said there was something else?

CALLER: Yes; as if that wasn't enough. My account shows that £107.27 was paid to a company called Pan Express. I don't know who this is …

OPERATOR: Let's have a look. Well, … it is genuine.

CALLER: I can assure you it's not mine.

OPERATOR: It was made on the evening of the 12th of May. Maybe it's a restaurant bill you forgot about?

CALLER: There's no way that … . Oh wait, hold on …

OPERATOR: Yes?

CALLER: It's okay. I've just realized what it is. It is a restaurant bill. Erm … the name of the company is different from the name of the restaurant. My mistake. I'm sorry.

OPERATOR: That's okay. Was there anything else?

CALLER: I don't know if I dare …

OPERATOR: What is it anyway?

CALLER: Mmm. Well, it's mmm … the amount of interest seems to have gone up.

OPERATOR: Mmmm. If you look at your statement for April, you'll see that the rate went down from 16.27% to 14.99% that month.

CALLER: Oh, yes you're right.

OPERATOR: Was that everything?

CALLER: Yes. Basically, it is.

OPERATOR: Okay.

CALLER: And can you check my payment?

OPERATOR: Oh yes. I'll do it. Can I phone you back?

CALLER: I'll be at home for the next two hours. I have to leave at 11.

OPERATOR: Right. What's your number?

CALLER: 020 7989 7182.

OPERATOR: Hold on 020 7979.

CALLER: No, it's 7989 and then 7182.

OPERATOR: So it's 020 7989 7182.

CALLER: Yes. That's it.

OPERATOR: Okay. I'll phone you straight back.

CALLER: Thanks. Bye.

TEST ONE SECTION 2

Questions 11–13

PRESENTER: And now let's hear what Mr Gold has to say about kicking the habit of smoking. It was connected with wanting to change your life and your desire to become an actor. Is that right, Mr Gold?

MR GOLD: Mm. Yes.

PRESENTER: So can you tell our listeners a bit more about how you managed to give up?

MR GOLD: Mm. Well, I enrolled on a variety of evening courses, where I found I wasn't able to do the warm-up sessions. Bending down to touch my toes made me breathless. Even though I hated to admit it, the problem wasn't so much my sitting around all the time, but my 15 to 20 a day smoking habit.

If I'd been able to limit myself to three or four cigarettes a day, there'd have been no problem, but I was seriously addicted. And I'm talking about waking up at 3 a.m. dying for a cigarette, or, in the days before 24-hour shopping, driving across London at night to buy a packet of cigarettes when I ran out. But above all, my addiction meant making sure I never ran out, at the expense of everything else, including necessities.

PRESENTER: So what did you do?

MR GOLD: The thought of all my past attempts to give up just wouldn't go away. This was something that had constantly been on my mind, especially first thing in the morning with the chest pains, coughing fits and headaches. Not to mention the frequent colds and throat infections. But I couldn't imagine life without smoking.

I also enjoyed my life. But the thing I longed for most was to escape the trap of a job I was bored with. I knew what I wanted, and I understood something else too. This time I was going to keep my little plan a secret.

Questions 14–20

On 1st July I managed to get through 24 hours without a single cigarette. The next day I got to 48 hours. Then I aimed for a hundred, five hundred, a thousand. Easy! It was my own little private game, and I was winning it. If anyone mentioned they hadn't seen me smoking I simply said I was cutting down. I had to be sure of success. Eventually, a month passed and I felt safe enough to 'come out'. I'd lost count of the number of hours I'd gone without a cigarette. All I suffered was a couple of bad headaches and then I was set for my most healthy year ever – not one single cold for over twelve months.

I now realize that the secret of my success was to look upon this as an exciting adventure, a way of helping me to become an actor. And because nobody knew what I was up to, I never once feared the accusation of having no willpower if I failed. With the right attitude, the whole thing turned out to be a lot easier than expected. I finally did get into much better physical shape, go to drama school and become a professional actor.

PRESENTER: Very interesting indeed! I'm sure we all wish we had Mr Gold's determination! Well, thank you very much Mr Gold, and I hope our listeners will learn from the experience you and our other guests have talked to us about today, and perhaps find their own road to success.

TEST ONE SECTION 3

Questions 21–23

TUTOR: Ah, Frances and Steve, Hi. Now, before we start the tutorial … am I right in thinking that you haven't heard about Lorraine?

FRANCES: No. What about her?

TUTOR: Mmm, she's already left.

STEVE: What?

FRANCES: Well, she hasn't told anyone!

TUTOR: You sound surprised. Weren't you half expecting it?

FRANCES: Yes, but she could at least have told us, though. We've been on the course together for the past three years and it would have been nice to know. She always was the sort to keep herself to herself.

STEVE: Yes. I know what you mean. Did she give any reason?

TUTOR: Well, she got that job.

FRANCES: What??

TUTOR: Yes, and she's been given permission to leave as there's only a week to go before the end of the course. But she'll be back for the exam week.

FRANCES: Oh, well. We'll just have to catch her on the mobile after the class.

TUTOR: She's gone back to Wales first.

FRANCES: Oh, dear.

STEVE: We'll get hold of her on the mobile.

TUTOR: She did say that it might not be possible to contact her for a couple of weeks.

FRANCES: Oh, okay. If that is what she wants.

Questions 24–30

TUTOR: Right. To work! We're here to look at your assessment marks for your course work. I take it you haven't seen them yet.

FRANCES/STEVE: No, not yet.

TUTOR: Well, you'll both be pleased. In fact, very pleased.

STEVE: Yes?

TUTOR: Frances. You have come out with the top mark in the year.

FRANCES: Oh!

TUTOR: You have, in fact, got a starred First.

STEVE: Wow.

TUTOR: Aren't you pleased, Frances?

FRANCES: Yes. I'm just speechless.

STEVE: And what about me?

TUTOR: Well, Steve, you got a First as well.

STEVE: I don't believe it!

TUTOR: You might have done even better, but there were a few faults with the 5,000 word project you did on traffic management.

STEVE: And what about the book review we had to do?

TUTOR: Yours was, I can safely say, the best we have ever had.

STEVE: You're kidding!

TUTOR: I'm not. In fact, you have won the departmental prize for the piece. It is a pity really that your project wasn't of the same calibre.

STEVE: It's still not bad at all, though. Is it?

TUTOR: It certainly isn't. What do you think were the faults with your project?

STEVE: I just wasn't very happy with the conclusion and I got myself in a bit of a twist with the argument about road pricing.

TUTOR: By and large, your overall conclusions were okay and I would say that your thoughts on road pricing were quite original. The problem was more with the actual end. It was a bit disappointing. You started off well, but then it ended rather suddenly as if you got fed up with it.

STEVE: Yes. I did kind of stop fairly abruptly. I couldn't think of much to say, even though I knew it was important.

TUTOR: Yes. That section needed a bit more work on it. But as I said, by and large it was very good. And Frances. Your project was excellent, so much so that we think you should take it further and perhaps do a PhD or at least an MPhil. What do you think?

FRANCES: I hadn't really thought about it. I've just been concerned with getting through this final year and getting all the course work and exams out of the way.

TUTOR: I can understand that, but I do think that you ought to consider it seriously. If you perform as well in your exams as in your project work you are on course for a first.

FRANCES: Do you think that I'd get funding for it?

TUTOR: Well, any grant will be discretionary, but you have as good a chance as anyone else – I'd even say a much better one.

FRANCES: Mmm.

TUTOR: If you do get a first, it will be the only one we've had in this department for three years. And I'd be happy to be your supervisor.

FRANCES: Thanks! I'd like that. Do you think I should start applying for it now or wait until after the exams?

TUTOR: I think you must really start thinking about it as soon as you can. And Steve, what about you? Have you thought about going on to do research?

STEVE: I have thought about it, but I have a job lined up if I get a good degree and, quite honestly, I am fed up with not having enough money to do the things I would like to do.

TUTOR: I can understand that. Is there anything that either of you would like to talk about?

STEVE: Yeah. I have a couple of things I'd like to ask, if you don't mind.

TUTOR: Okay. We have roughly twenty minutes left. So Steve, would you like to go first?

STEVE: Right , ammm ...

TEST ONE SECTION 4

Questions 31–33

Good morning, my name is Dr Mervin Forest and I specialize in management techniques and training. I've been invited here today to talk to you about the cost to the economy of bad management … and what I would like to dwell on first is an area that has recently been exercising everyone and that is coercion in the workplace, or to put it more simply, bullying.

It has been estimated that bullying at work costs the British economy up to four billion pounds a year in lost working time and in legal fees. And with the problem apparently on the increase, it is time that managers took on board what is happening. I would like to think that what is perceived as bullying is nothing more than lack of experience, insecurity or lack of awareness on the part of managers, and not a conscious effort to attack someone, but that is perhaps a case of, of … my being naïve, or over-hopeful.

Before we break up into groups to look at the first task on the handout you've got, I'd like to give you a start with some of the main bullying methods that have been identified so far. Basically, what I'm going to do here is to give you examples of one or two points. Can you all read the OHP clearly? Yes? Right. Off we go.

Questions 34–40

The first item on the list is giving people tasks which managers themselves cannot do and which are, therefore, impossible to achieve. This is, in fact, a very common strategy used by managers to 'manage' their subordinates. It gives certain people a false sense of security as they watch others failing while they try to achieve the goals set. Another simple bullying technique is constantly moving the goalposts, especially when one's employees are in the middle of a task! This is not bad management; it is just plain stupid. All targets and goals set should be easily achieved within a realistic time-scale.

Sending memos to someone else criticizing the performance of a task where the individual has no way of replying is another common technique; especially when the manager concerned does not reply or makes it impossible for subordinates to contact him or her by not answering the telephone or not replying to e-mails. This is not the style of a sound manager, but rather the antics of someone with emotional problems. If you behave like that, don't expect your staff to respect you.

And now the technological bully. It is interesting how all tools designed to help can be turned into dangerous weapons. The 'urgent e-mail' bully is fast becoming a problem in the office. Employees turn on their computers to be faced with a string of badly worded e-mails, making instant and often unrealistic demands, which reveal the hysteria mode of management. Have you ever felt a sense of dread before looking at your e-mail, even your personal messages? All companies should develop a company strategy whereby there is an e-mail code of practice, with offensive messages being forwarded to a designated person for appropriate action.

I would now like you to break up into groups and brainstorm other bullying techniques which you think you may have experienced and, perhaps, if you are honest, which you have been party to. I can think of at least nine more bullying strategies. I would also like you to consider ways in which you think that each of the techniques on your list can be countered.

Is everyone clear as to what the task is? Yes? Okay. You have got twenty minutes to do this.

TEST TWO SECTION 1

Questions 1–5

DAD: Hello? 992846.

HANNAH: Dad? Is that you?

DAD: Hannah?

HANNAH: Dad. I'm phoning ...

DAD: The line isn't very clear.

HANNAH: Yes, I know, I'm on a mobile and the signal isn't very good. I'll see if I can move ... is that any better?

DAD: Yes. That's much better. Just don't move.

HANNAH: I'll try not to.

[Repeat]

DAD: Have you found a place to live yet?

HANNAH: Yes! I think I have at last.

DAD: Wonderful!

HANNAH: I'm relieved, because I'm fed up looking. I didn't think it was going to take me three weeks.

DAD: It hasn't been easy for you. I suppose it's the beginning of the academic year and you have all the new students looking for places as well.

HANNAH: Yes, that's one reason. But this place is also full of new technology companies and there are lots of young people looking for somewhere to live. And you know what that means?

DAD: Higher rents as well.

HANNAH: Yes. Much higher.

DAD: Well, tell me, how much is it?

HANNAH: It isn't cheap for this area. It's 400 pounds a month.

DAD: That is much more than you had expected.

HANNAH: Yes, it is, but I can't face looking any more. I want a place where I can put my things, instead of living out of a suitcase. I don't want to stay in this hotel any longer.

DAD: I guess not. So what's the new place like?

HANNAH: Oh, it's really, really nice.

DAD: Oh, good.

HANNAH: It's in a very quiet street. It's a second-floor flat with one double bedroom, a large living room, kitchen and toilet and bathroom.

DAD: Sounds very nice.

HANNAH: Oh it is. And guess what?

DAD: Yes?

HANNAH: It's got a small roof terrace looking on to the garden at the back.

DAD: Great.

HANNAH: And it's big enough to have my plants and a small table and chairs.

DAD: Brilliant.

Questions 6–10

DAD: Now, what's the address?

HANNAH: It's 22b Whitehart Road.

DAD: 22e.

HANNAH: No, 22b. B for ... banana.

DAD: Right. And it's Whitehart Road.

HANNAH: Yes.

DAD: And the postcode?

HANNAH: You know, I don't think ... I've ... got it.

DAD: Okay.

HANNAH: No ... here it is. It's EX15 9RJ

DAD: This line is bad. Is that EX50?

HANNAH: No it's EX15.

DAD: Okay. I don't think I know the road.

HANNAH: It's a side road. But you do know the area because it's off Garret Lane.

DAD: Oh right. Which end?

HANNAH: The other end from the stadium.

DAD: So it won't be too noisy then.

HANNAH: You can still hear it from here when there's a match on.

DAD: Mmm. When are we going to see you?

HANNAH: Well, I was going to come down on Friday evening after work. And then we could bring my things by van on Saturday afternoon. I want to move all of my stuff out to give you and Mum more space.

DAD: We'll need to hire a van then.

HANNAH: It's okay. I'll pay for it.

DAD: No. No. Don't worry. It'll be a gift from your Mum and me.

HANNAH: Oh, Dad. It's okay I ...

DAD: No, I won't hear of it. We'll pay.

HANNAH: Oh, all right. Thanks, Dad.

DAD: And if you're taking everything we might need to hire a container lorry.

HANNAH: Oh, Dad!!

DAD: I'm only joking.

HANNAH: I know.

DAD: I'll hire the van for the Saturday then. I can pick it up first thing in the morning.

HANNAH: Right.

DAD: And then return it in the evening.

HANNAH: Are you sure you don't want to stay overnight?

DAD: No, I'd best get back the same day. You know what your Mum's like. She'll only worry. If I remember rightly, it's about three hours by road?

HANNAH: Yes, roughly.

DAD: Well, if we leave by lunch time, we'll be there mid-afternoon.

HANNAH: Okay.

DAD: Then a couple of hours to unpack.

HANNAH: Then ...

DAD: We could go to a nice restaurant round the corner.

HANNAH: Definitely. My treat!

DAD: You're on. But I'll have to be away by about seven-thirtyish.

HANNAH: Okay.

DAD: Right then. Ahm ... Mum wants to have a word. I'll see you Friday.

HANNAH: Bye, Dad.

DAD: I'll hand you over to her ... bye.

TEST TWO   SECTION 2

Questions 11–14

And now for our main headlines on Southern Local News for today. First of all, the report relating to the proposed motorway and other developments around the village of Tartlesbury was published this morning. And, as has been expected, it has created quite a lot of interest. The new motorway will pass along the north side of the village, crossing the River Teeme less than half a kilometre from the well-known beauty spot, Streeve Ford, to the north-east of the village. The motorway will cut the village off from the Ford, where many children play.

But that is not the end of it. There are also plans to build a thousand houses on farmland west of the village. And on top of that there are proposals to build an industrial estate for new technology companies on the site of the old steel works on the edge of the village. A new centre with a swimming pool and a very wide range of sports facilities, and a large supermarket with other shops are also planned next to the housing estate.

Questions 15–18

Mr Jones, a local farmer we spoke to early today, is strongly against the plans. But the local council is pushing for them to be adopted in full. They say that new housing is needed in the area and that it is an opportunity to take advantage of government grants for setting up new technology developments. The Mayor, Mr Funn, says: 'We must make every effort to do our part for the economy of the country and for the local people. This is a golden opportunity to put Tartlesbury on the map.'

Reactions to Mr Funn's comments have been quick to come. Surprisingly, when we contacted the spokesman of the local conservation group, he was very much for the planned developments. But not all the local groups support the scheme. And, unlike the Mayor, the local MP Mrs Wright is very much against the planned developments.

Mr Khan, a local shopkeeper, had this to say: 'People are absolutely horrified at what is being proposed here. This is just a chance for some people to make money quickly. But I can assure you that if they think that local people are going to be a walkover, they have another think coming. Of course, we welcome the jobs that the new technology park will bring, but we feel that the large increase in housing and the proposed motorway will destroy the character of the area.'

I think this is a debate that is going to run on for quite some time and we here on Local News will keep you informed.

Questions 19–20

And now for something quite different. This year's exam results have just come out and there are a lot of happy faces out there. It would seem that the number of young people going on to university from the local College in Upton, which is not far from Tartlesbury, has increased by 25% this year. All those who have applied to go to university or into teacher-training colleges have found places. This is the first time that there has been a 100% success rate at the College. We spoke earlier to the Principal of the College, who said she was very proud of all those who had achieved their aims and she wished them every success in the future.

There will be another news bulletin at 11 p.m. and for now it's back to more music from around the world.

TEST TWO SECTION 3

Questions 21–25

DR WOODHAM: So, Pamela, here's your essay. And Carl, you've already got yours back. Anything you want to ask or any comments?

CARL: Can you just go over again for us how the marks for our essays go towards our final grade?

DR: Well, mmm, over the year you are meant to write five main essays for this course.

CARL: Yes.

DR: And each essay's marked out of 20, which gives you a total of 100 marks.

CARL: Yes?

DR: This course work makes up 50% of your marks for the year, with the other 50% coming from the written exam.

CARL: Right. So the five essays contribute to 50% of our final grade for the year.

DR: Yes.

CARL: You gave me 18 out of 20 for this essay, which gives me a total of 9% towards my final grade for the year.

DR: Mmm, and …

PAMELA: And with 14 for this one, I've got 7%.

DR: Yes, Pamela. Does that clarify it?

PAMELA: Yes.

CARL: Mmm. Yes.

PAMELA: We did have it explained to us at the beginning of the course.

CARL: When?

PAMELA: In the first tutorial.

DR: Okay. I think we had better move on now. About your last essay, have either of you any questions or comments?

Questions 26–30

CARL: You gave me 18 for this paper. What was the big difference between this piece and the previous one? I actually thought the first one was better!

DR: Well, there was quite a marked difference.

CARL: Really?

DR: Yes. It looked as if you had actually done quite a bit of research. You had quite a lot of relevant examples, especially on the historical side. You even found some information that I was not even aware of! Your sources were also very sound. And on top of that, your answer was very well organized indeed and the writing style was very elegant.

CARL: Oh. Thank you very much!

DR: I must say that it was the best piece of writing for a paper that we've seen for quite some time.

CARL: I have to say, though, it took me a very long time to put it together.

PAMELA: How long?

CARL: At least two weeks.

DR: But it was well worth it.

CARL: Can I just ask you if it is possible to rewrite the first essay of the term? It's really brought my average down.

DR: I'm sorry, but it's impossible.

CARL: Is there no way to do it?

DR: I'm afraid not.

CARL: Okay. Right. I'll just have to try to do better than average on the others.

DR: And Pamela?

PAMELA: Well, to be honest, on the whole I am happy with my marks.

DR: Again, your research was very good. And you gave quite a long list of source material, which was very good.

PAMELA: I spent quite a lot of time on this essay, more than the others.

DR: Well, again, it shows.

PAMELA: What about the organization? I was a bit worried about that.

DR: Your organization, I have to say, was excellent.

PAMELA: Oh!

DR: But as regards your style ...

PAMELA: Yes?

DR: It is slightly too informal here and there. I think you need to tighten this up a little.

PAMELA: Mmm, okay. I only wish I'd put a bit more effort into the first one as well now. But I would like to know how I can get my marks up even higher. What do I have to do, specifically?

DR: Well, your work could do with being more thoroughly checked. You have quite a few spelling mistakes.

PAMELA: Yes, I know. If it's anything, I think it's the computer.

DR: Mhmmm?

PAMELA: Well, I am not very good at typing, two fingers really, and when I finish something like this I find it difficult, even depressing, to go over it carefully again.

DR: But it's affecting your marks.

PAMELA: Mmmmm.

DR: Your previous essay was much better than this one. Sometimes, it's difficult to follow what's being said because of the frequency of mistakes. A couple of years ago the university authorities would have been more lenient. But now they are very hot on presentation and have been coming down heavily on things like grammar and spelling.

PAMELA: Mmmmm.

DR: In fact, I am obliged to deduct marks from every piece of work which is not handed in fairly free of mistakes.

TEST TWO SECTION 4

Questions 31–35

Good afternoon, my name is Dr Charles Butt and I shall be giving you a series of lectures on productivity and work practices over the coming weeks. There will be ten lectures in the mornings as part of this course and, in addition, there will be three lectures in the evenings from six to eight which will be given by outside speakers.

I would like first to look at a recent report on life at work. The report shows that the average British worker takes less than half an hour for lunch, 27 minutes to be precise, and that sick leave is on the increase. The drop in the length of time spent on lunch was nine minutes when compared to last year, down from 36 minutes. According to the report, this is the first time that the average lunch break has fallen below half an hour.

As regards sick leave, you can see that the average figure is ten days per year, that's up by one day in

2002 compared to 2001. While physical illness was given as the most common reason for absence in the case of non-manual workers, stress was the most common cause of long-term absence. It's worth noting here that nine out of ten workers claim that stress is a problem in their organization and that eight out of ten bosses are feeling more stressed than ever before. I would just like to say here that we will be looking at the stress in work and study at a later date. And we will be looking particularly at ways of dealing with it in studying, particularly for exams. You can see from the calendar that Professor Appleyard will be giving a lecture on this topic the week after next.

The report also says that just below 50% of workers claim that they were taking less time off for holidays than they were entitled to. I am not sure that this will be believed by the employers. Previous surveys have suggested that about one-third of days that have been taken by workers as days off sick were regarded by bosses as not being the result of genuine illness. Some more hard data is required to corroborate both these claims.

Questions 36–40

All this suggests that employers are driving their workers too hard. The effects of over-working mean that workers are now being stretched beyond their limits both physically and mentally. This is borne out by the increase in sick leave. However, looked at from the employers' point of view, the picture may not be the same. Employers say that workers protest too much, but bearing in mind the data about the number of bosses feeling much more stress than before, we need to think about this carefully. It's interesting to note that productivity has gone up in many areas of industry. In 2001, the local car plant had one of the sharpest increases in average productivity with the number of vehicles per employee rising by over 30% a year. A new assembly line came into operation at the beginning of 2002, affecting productivity which increased to the 100-vehicles-per-worker mark by the end of the year. This is a stunning achievement for an industry which was not long ago considered to be collapsing.

It would be interesting to do a survey of the work life at the plant. Those of you who have opted to do the project and reduce the number of essays you have to do may want to look into this. Please see me at the end of the lecture. Right now, let us move on ... .

TEST THREE   SECTION 1

Questions 1–5

CAROLINE: Hi, Matt. Right on time.

MATT: Have you been waiting long?

CAROLINE: Mmm, five minutes.

MATT: The buses were held up on the High Street; otherwise, I would have been early.

CAROLINE: Yeah. There is something wrong with them today.

[Repeat]

MATT: Yeah. I think so. Okay. What shall we do? Shall we go and have a coffee?

CAROLINE: Yeah. That would be nice. There's that place on the corner over there. It does really nice coffee and cakes and things and at this time it is usually very quiet, so we'll be able to talk.

MATT: Okay. Let's go there then.

CAROLINE: So, when's the party going to be?

MATT: Well, it has to be at the end of September before we all leave for university.

CAROLINE: We have plenty of time then. We don't go for another five weeks, do we?

MATT: Mmm. Well, we haven't really got that much time, if you think about it. There are only a couple of weeks at the beginning of September when all of us are around.

CAROLINE: Oh yes, I forgot. Nasrin, Phil and Nikki and all that lot have gone off on holiday.

MATT: And I am away for two weeks from tomorrow.

CAROLINE: So, what does that leave us then?

MATT: As far as I know, we are all here between the 19th and the 30th of September. Will Sandra be around then? I know that she has a whole string of family birthdays at that time and she might not be available.

CAROLINE: Mmm. Well, let's make a note of that and we can contact her about it.

MATT: Okay. Shall we settle for the 21st of September then?

CAROLINE: What day is the 21st?

MATT: It's a Saturday. Is that okay?

CAROLINE: That's fine.

Questions 6–10

MATT: And now for the tricky bit. Where are we going to hold it?

CAROLINE: Well, I spoke to Nikki last week and she volunteered her place as they have a huge house and garden.

MATT: Oh, fantastic. Will her parents be around?

CAROLINE: Yeah, I think so, but she said they won't mind.

MATT: Oh, right. Well, my parents wouldn't like it at all.

CAROLINE: Nor mine!

MATT: But is it definite?

CAROLINE: Yes. When I spoke to her, she said it was definitely on. I'll just have to confirm the dates with her. We thought it would be one weekend in September, so I'll just have to make sure that that one is okay. One thing Nikki suggested, we could have a daytime party as we could be outside if the weather is fine.

MATT: Oh, wow! How far out does she live?

CAROLINE: It's not that far. Do you know where West Road crosses the bridge?

MATT: Yeah?

CAROLINE: It's the first house on the right with that huge drive up to the front door.

MATT: Oh, right. I know exactly where it is. The road is off the A33 and runs north, then over the bridge and first on the right. I know it. The place is amazing. You know it has a big swimming pool? Does everyone know where she lives?

CAROLINE: Most of her friends do, but not all. But it doesn't matter, as we can put this map Nikki sent me in with the invitation.

MATT: How shall we do the invitation?

CAROLINE: We can do it on the computer. I can scan the map and we'll put it all on to an A4 page.

MATT: Is this the address? Can I just write the address down? It's 93 West Road. And I'll take the phone number. It's 4 7 7 1 3 0.

CAROLINE: Right. There's one other thing.

MATT: Yes?

CAROLINE: We are all giving ten pounds towards refreshments and food. There will probably be a barbecue. Do you think that's enough?

MATT: Oh, right. Yeah that's fine.

CAROLINE: And everyone will have to help tidy up afterwards, including the boys!

TEST THREE   SECTION 2

Questions 11–13

TUTOR: Good morning, everyone.

STUDENTS: Good morning.

TUTOR: My name is Dr Russell and I am your tutor for philosophy this year. I think we are all here. Let's see, five, six, seven. Yes, that's everyone. Before we look at the three lectures you've had on philosophy this week, I would just like to run through a few things about what you can expect of me as tutor and what in turn we expect of you.

As for myself, my function as tutor is to help you in all things relating to your work in the philosophy course. The help that I am able to give is, of course, mainly academic. For personal matters, I can refer you to other support services in the university, ranging from counselling to, um … welfare. One thing that I would point out is that, if you feel that you need to talk to someone, no matter how insignificant it is, don't leave it. Oh, and the last thing is, if you do need to make an appointment, the times are listed on the door of my room. You just write your name in a time slot. But I would point out that the appointment slots get booked up quite quickly. If it's urgent, catching me between sessions is the best idea. That way we can sort something out quickly. Ahm … no questions?

Questions 14–20

Okay. As regards you as students, the tutorials are voluntary; you are not obliged to attend, but you are encouraged to do so. Last year, for the first time, a register was kept of students attending lectures and, this year, tutors are being asked to keep a register of tutorial attendance. This is not a formal register and not all tutors will be doing it, but in the Philosophy department all of us have chosen to keep registers. Another point that's being emphasized this year is punctuality. When we did exit questionnaires we found that people arriving late for tutorials and lectures was the single most annoying thing for the majority of students. I would therefore ask you to try to be on time for the tutorials, and for all your other classes for that matter.

As regards the tutorials themselves, we will have a review of the philosophy lectures of the week before with the discussion being led by one of you each week. There is, of course, some planning involved, but you should rely primarily on the notes you made at the lectures. This will not take up the whole of the 90 minutes allocated to the tutorial. For the rest of the time, we will look at a particular philosopher, period or concept, for which you will be expected to do some preparation each week. This will range from reading about a particular individual or concept to preparing a brief outline on a subject of your choice. How much you put into this depends on you, but we are not expecting in-depth analysis at this stage. Um … are there any questions so far?

STUDENT: I'd just like to ask whether the work we do in the tutorials counts towards our continuous assessment and, if so, how much?

TUTOR: I was just coming on to that point. All the work you do in the way of essays and project work that is graded counts towards your continuous assessment grades. The mini-presentations and lecture discussions will not be graded but, obviously, as time goes on, these activities will, I hope, have an impact on your work and hence your scores. Does that answer your question?

STUDENT: Basically, yes, but what about … .

TEST THREE   SECTION 3

Questions 21–24

MARK: I've never written an essay of more than 1,500 words before, Anne.

ANNE: Me neither, Mark. And it scares me.

MARK: Oh, I wouldn't worry. We'll just have to pretend it's four essays of 1,500 words and join them together!!

ANNE: It says here in the assignment notes Dr Brightwell gave us that we're to write between 5,000 and 6,000 words on some aspect of students' attitudes backed up by our own research which we present in the form of tables, graphs, charts or whatever and supported by reference to the list of books she gave us. I didn't realize there had been so many social science books written about students.

MARK: Oh, yeah. There are a lot. Mmm. And the questionnaire?

ANNE: Yes. Mmm, we have to, mmm, prepare a questionnaire to gather our own data for the graphs etc. and hand it in to Dr Brightwell in draft form in, mmm, two weeks' time.

MARK: Two weeks?

ANNE: That's what she said and what it says here; she says that it's better to have it checked before we go on to collect the information and start the writing.

MARK: Suppose she's right. We'd better get started then. But she didn't say how we were going to put the questionnaire together; does it say anything in the notes?

ANNE: Nope. It only says that we're limited to four sides of A4. And no more than 50 questions.

MARK: If that's the case it's not that bad.

Questions 25–30

MARK: So, how are we going to do it?

ANNE: Well, first we need to know who we're aiming it, then decide how many questions we are going to ask. I think we could have about 40 questions maximum. I don't think there's any real need to go up to the 50 limit.

MARK: Mmm.

ANNE: And I think we should keep the questions themselves very simple.

MARK: Don't worry, in my case they will be!

ANNE: We could have a mixture of question types, like multiple-choice questions, Yes/No and Agree/Disagree with boxes for people to tick. If people are asked to write down anything, it's unlikely they will fill it in.

MARK: So, are we going to give this questionnaire out to people to hand in or are we going to just stop and ask them around the campus or on the street?

ANNE: Mmmm, I don't really know. Did she say anything about this? Mmm. No, she didn't, and there is nothing in these notes she gave us either.

MARK: I think we ought to give them out.

ANNE: Okay.

MARK: Anyway, it won't affect the way we design the questionnaire.

ANNE: We're both doing it on different subjects, but there's nothing wrong with pooling our ideas about the mechanism of the questionnaire.

MARK: No. None. What are you doing your project on?

ANNE: I have been thinking about doing something around the subject of, mmm, how aware students are of world affairs. People think that we are all up to date, but I very much doubt it. It would also be interesting to compare students in different years. And you?

MARK: I'm doing something on health and sport and whether students are more, or less, active since they came to university.

ANNE: Sounds interesting. As the questionnaires can be anonymous, I'll fill in your first questionnaire for you, but I am sure you won't be surprised by my answers.

MARK: Somehow, I don't think so!

ANNE: I suggest we put together about 20 … or 25 questions each, and then meet tomorrow or the day after and compare them?

MARK: Are you going to type yours up?

ANNE: Yeah. Then I can come round to your place and we can work on them. You've got a laptop, haven't you?

MARK: Yes. And I've got some new design software so we can play around with the layout.

ANNE: Brilliant! Are you any good at doing charts and things?

MARK: I know how to do simple things on the computer, but we'll sort something out.

ANNE: Okay.

MARK: I feel much better about all this now. It doesn't seem quite as bad as I first thought.

ANNE: No. Don't worry, we'll get it done.

TEST THREE   SECTION 4

Questions 31–35

Good morning, my name is Professor Sarah Lennon, and I am here today to talk to you about the works of one of the greatest writers in the English language, Charles Dickens. He wrote many books and, if we bear in mind that there are over 2,000 characters in his stories, we can get an idea of the complexity of his work. I've selected one novel from your reading list that I would like to talk about to illustrate his genius, namely, *Dombey and Son*. But before we look at this work in earnest, I thought it might be a good idea to have a quick look at his life, and also at a few of the major events that happened during his lifetime, so that we can try to put his writing into perspective.

Dickens was born on the 7th of February, 1812, at the time when his father was working in Portsmouth dockyard. His father was transferred to London in 1814. To help give us a picture of the time Dickens was born into, it's worth noting that, in 1814 when Dickens was two, the first efficient steam locomotive was constructed in Newcastle-upon-Tyne. Then in 1817, the year that Queen Victoria was born and Waterloo Bridge in London was opened, the Dickens family moved away from London. And to give Dickens' life a literary perspective, in the following year, works by other famous English writers were published: Jane Austen's *Northanger Abbey* and *Persuasion*, Mary Shelley's *Frankenstein* and Scott's *The Heart of Midlothian*.

When Dickens was almost ten, his family circumstances changed and in 1822 the family moved back to London. In 1824, John Dickens was arrested for debt and imprisoned in the Marshalsea near London Bridge in London. This event had a profound effect on Dickens' writing. From 1827, Charles Dickens had various jobs as solicitor's clerk, freelance reporter and newspaper reporter.

Questions 36–40

In December 1833, Dickens had his first story, *A Dinner at Poplar Wall*, published in the *Monthly Magazine*; in the same year, the SS *Royal William* became the first vessel to cross the Atlantic Ocean by steam alone. In 1836, two important events happened. Dickens published the first series of *Sketches by Boz* and the publishers, Chapman and Hall, suggested his first novel, the *Pickwick Papers*. In April of the same year, the second major event took place: Dickens married Catherine Hogarth. And in 1837, the year that Queen Victoria became Queen of England and Samuel B Morse developed telegraph, the novel *Oliver Twist* began publication in Bentley's *Miscellany* in 24 monthly instalments. You may not be aware that serialization like this was common in Dickens' time. In the subsequent year, that is in 1838, the serialization of *Nicholas Nickleby* started and appeared in 20 instalments.

Dickens' novel *The Old Curiosity Shop* began serialization in 1840. This was the year the first postage stamp, the penny post, was brought in by Rowland Hill and the year the first bicycle was produced. The next major publication for Dickens was in 1842 when the first part of *Martin Chuzzlewit* appeared, and in 1848 *Dombey and Son* was published.

Now, do you have any questions before we go on to look at this work in some depth? No?

TEST FOUR   SECTION 1

Questions 1–6

AUTOMATED PHONE: Thank you for calling Car Line. So that we can best help you, can you please press the star button on your phone now. Thank you.

AUTOMATED PHONE: Now choose one of the following four options by pressing the buttons on your telephone. Press 1 if you would like to make a car reservation. Press 2 if you would like to talk to someone about a car reservation. Press 3 if you would … . Please hold while we put you through to one of our assistants.

[repeat]

MELANIE: Good morning, Melanie speaking. How can I help you?

MR MAXINE: My name is Mr Maxine and I booked a car several days ago to be picked up from Heathrow airport in London. And I'd like to change the booking.

MELANIE: I see. Have you got a reference?

MR MAXINE: Yes. I have it here somewhere on a piece of paper. Ah, here it is. It's A for Alpha, C for Charlie, F for Foxtrot, Y for ...

MELANIE: Year.

MR MAXINE: Yes. The number 15 – one, five – A for Alpha and G for Go.

MELANIE: Let's see. Can I just check that? A C F Y 1 5 A G.

MR MAXINE: Yes.

MELANIE: Mr John Maxine.

MR MAXINE: Yes. That's it.

MELANIE: Okay. So how can I help you?

MR MAXINE: I booked a car for three days from this Friday at 6 p.m. to Monday at 6 p.m.

MELANIE: Yes. A manual.

MR MAXINE: I'd like to change it for a larger car and an automatic rather than a manual. And I'd also like to book it for five rather than three days.

MELANIE: Okay. Let's have a look. Mmm. We have an estate which is automatic.

MR MAXINE: Yes. That would be perfect.

MELANIE: There is a difference in price though.

MR MAXINE: For the extra two days?

MELANIE: Yes, but also for the size of the car. The estate is £15 more expensive per day than the saloon car you have already booked.

MR MAXINE: Okay. And how much extra is it altogether, then?

MELANIE: That makes it an extra £165.

MR MAXINE: Mm. It seems rather expensive. The last time I hired one it wasn't so much.

MELANIE: When was that?

MR MAXINE: Mm … several weeks ago.

MELANIE: I see …

Questions 7–10

MELANIE: Well, it's basically because the rates change daily according to the cars available. The estate is the last automatic we have for hire for that period. We have a manual estate, which is cheaper, if that would help?

MR MAXINE: No. It has to be an automatic.

MELANIE: Okay. Shall I debit your card for the extra £165?

MR MAXINE: Is it possible for me to pay the extra in cash when I pick up the car at the airport?

MELANIE: I'm afraid that isn't possible as there are no facilities for handling cash at that time of the day.

MR MAXINE: That seems odd.

MELANIE: It's because the money can't be banked in the evening and for security reasons no cash is held on the premises.

MR MAXINE: Okay. You can debit my card.

MELANIE: You'll have to give the number to me again.

MR MAXINE: Isn't it logged on the screen?

MELANIE: For security reasons it does not come up on the screen when we look at the booking. Any changes, and it has to be entered again.

MR MAXINE: I see. It's 3445 9911.

MELANIE: 3445 9911.

MR MAXINE: 4425.

MELANIE: 4425.

MR MAXINE: 7750.

MELANIE: 7750. Okay, that has now been authorized. Shall we send the receipt to your Park Vale address?

MR MAXINE: Yes, number 40.

MELANIE: Is there anything else I can help you with, Mr Maxine?

MR MAXINE: No, nothing else, thank you.

MELANIE: Have a nice trip.

MR MAXINE: Thank you. Goodbye.

TEST FOUR   SECTION 2

Questions 11–14

PRESENTER: And now for our Mystery Personality of the week and your chance to win one of our fabulous prizes. Last week's competition generated a huge response and the first five answers pulled out of the bag will receive £100 worth of sports clothes vouchers. And if you didn't win last week, here's another chance. And this week's prize is even bigger. We are giving away ten prizes of £250 worth of book, music and clothes vouchers to mark the first anniversary of the show on the air, so get your pens ready to take down the address details. Just write the name of the person you think is our Mystery Personality and send it to Mystery Draw at the address Marcia will give you in just a second. The address will be repeated at the end of the show for those of you who didn't get it. And so it's over to Marcia who will tell you a few tantalizing details about our mystery person this week.

MARCIA: Thanks, Mike. Well, here goes. Our mystery person this week is a very well-known footballer who plays for a famous club, and has also played for his national team. He is very talented and is enormously popular, especially for the part he played in a famous footballing victory. And two clues: he hasn't got a famous wife and he speaks French. If you think you know who it is, then pop the answer on a postcard and send it to Mystery Draw, PO Box 5110,

London SE1 5LE. That's PO Box 5110. And please don't forget to write your name and address, too. And now, it's back to Mike.

Questions 15–20

PRESENTER: Thank you, Marcia. Get those postcards in and make this a bumper anniversary draw. Now, if you remember, last week on the show we talked to the organizer of a new group set up to help young people up to the age of 20 to get involved in activities like horse-riding, tennis, scuba-diving, cycling or any form of sport which involves some kind of expense. John Tebbit, the organizer, rang us to say that the response to his appeal on the show was staggering. A large number of people both young and old have offered their services free as volunteers. The whole thing has been overwhelming. John said that they had also had numerous offers of help throughout the country to use facilities free of charge. As if that was not enough, they have received many donations, including several rather large gifts of more than £5,000! On behalf of John Tebbit and also of those who will benefit from the generous gifts to the trust, I would like to say thank you.

This week we are going to talk to a very unusual athlete indeed. Patrick, who is 20 years of age, has been wheelchair-bound for the past five years after a motorcycle accident left him paralysed from the waist down. This has not stopped this young man from getting out and about. He's an inspiration to all of us. Patrick has excelled in archery, beating the best in the field; so much so that he has won sponsorship from leading sports manufacturers which has now enabled him to devote more time to perfecting his skills. So, I would like to introduce you to Patrick who is going to tell us what this sponsorship means to him.

TEST FOUR   SECTION 3

Questions 21–24

ASTRID: Henry, don't you think Dr Adams' lecture was really very good? He could talk about the telephone directory and make it interesting.

HENRY: All his lectures are like that, Astrid. He's just one of those people. I wish we had him as our tutor.

ASTRID: I bet you that he is very demanding, though. Boris is in his tutorial group and agrees that he is a brilliant lecturer, but he puts them under a lot of pressure.

HENRY: Mmm, but don't you think that's good?

ASTRID: Perhaps, but I am glad to have Dr Adams as a lecturer. He's interesting and rather funny and puts just the right amount of pressure on people.

HENRY: Did you take lots of notes in the lecture?

ASTRID: Yes, actually I did; in fact, several pages. I didn't think I had taken so many.

HENRY: I was that busy listening to what was being said that I didn't take many notes. Can I photocopy yours?

ASTRID: I don't think that's such a good idea. You won't be able to read my handwriting and sometimes I write them in English and sometimes in Arabic.

HENRY: Oh, let's have a look. Wow! Your notes are so neat. There's not much Arabic.

ASTRID: There is on this page.

HENRY: Yes, there is. Dr Adams would be pleased to see this, especially given what he was talking about.

ASTRID: Don't you keep careful notes?

HENRY: Sometimes. It depends on the lecture. I don't think I'll forget Adams' lecture today, but some of the detail will fade.

Questions 25–30

ASTRID: I type up everything afterwards so you can have a copy then and you can fill in anything I have missed. I am not so good on the broader concepts. I am better when it comes to detail.

HENRY: Just what Adams was talking about!

ASTRID: Well, I am definitely a detail person. I need to have everything written down before I can get the concepts clear in my head.

HENRY: And I am the complete opposite. I find all the detail clutters up my mind and I get very frustrated, which was just what he was on about. He mentioned a book he had written.

ASTRID: He mentioned several.

HENRY: The one on space and the individual.

ASTRID: Yes, called *My Space*; it's on the book list.

HENRY: So it is. I think I'll get that out of the library or get my own copy.

ASTRID: Did you get what he said about spatial awareness? I didn't really.

HENRY: Yes, it was fascinating. I can't be as eloquent as Adams was, but I know several people who are frighteningly intelligent, but they have difficulty reading simple directions, even when getting to places that they know very well.

ASTRID: I find that difficult to understand. Everyone learns the way to walk to the shops and things like that.

HENRY: You mean just the way people learn spelling! You know people misspell words, make mistakes in countless areas of their lives, and going in the right direction is just the same. Remember what Adams said about the number of people who cannot tell left from right, north from south and so on. Do you know which way is north?

ASTRID: It's … mmm … that way.

HENRY: You see, I couldn't have told you that.

ASTRID: Really?

HENRY: I haven't a clue which way is which. That's why I am always getting lost when I go out on my bike. And put me in a completely new place and I am totally lost.

ASTRID: What about maps?

HENRY: I'm hopeless at reading them.

ASTRID: But then you're brilliant at writing essays and getting all the ideas down in the right order and I don't know where to start!

HENRY: Again, just what Adams was talking about! What we need to do is combine our skills; you teach me to cope with detail and I'll teach you how to string concepts together.

ASTRID: Okay, we can do that.

HENRY: Which way is the library?

ASTRID: It's … . You're making fun of me!

TEST FOUR   SECTION 4

Questions 31–36

Good morning again, ladies and gentlemen, and in case you've forgotten, my name is Dr North from the Marine Habitat Research Unit at the University and I'm going to continue from the lecture that I gave a fortnight ago on humankind's relationship with the sea from a historical point of view and also on attitudes to different types of fishing. In today's talk, I would like to focus on the current problems in the fishing industry in Europe and, in particular, the present scarcity of marine fish. As with the last lecture, I have placed a book list, a few relevant articles and a copy of this lecture on the department website.

A statistic to begin with. Since the 1970s, stocks of the most heavily fished species have fallen on average by 90%. And why has this happened? Well, there is a chain of events which begins with the demographic changes that have taken place in the world over the last century. During this time, the world population has grown at a phenomenal rate with efficient and heavy fishing, which is technology-driven, meeting the increasing demands for food. As a consequence, many fishing stocks in the European waters from the Atlantic to the North Sea and the Mediterranean are now on the verge of collapse. But the problem is not restricted to European waters. It's a situation that is all too clear all around the world. Fish stocks in the Pacific Ocean, for example, are now on the verge of collapse due to a combination of over fishing and natural changes in ocean ecology. And there's another reason behind the increased demand for fish and that is the changes in the eating patterns of different countries. Certain countries have a long tradition of fishing, for example, the southern European countries, but eating patterns have changed in countries like the United Kingdom, where fish was once considered as food for the poor rather than the rich. People have been turning to fish as a cheap and healthy alternative to meat, driving up demand and depleting stocks. Food scares like BSE and foot-and-mouth disease have also driven people away from eating meat, which again is invariably replaced by fish.

Questions 37–40

Another important reason is that a sizeable proportion of the catch from modern trawlers or fishing boats is thrown away. Nets quite often land fish that are not wanted and which are thrown back into the sea, dead. Discarded nets and other traps are responsible for the deaths of many fish. Our seas, like the rest of our environment, are littered with rubbish which also destroys lots of fish. And fish are also being changed by the chemicals dumped into the oceans as well as by over fishing so the size of certain species is decreasing. More then have to be fished to produce a decent catch.

And the solution? Well, there has to be more than one answer to the problem. Fish farms provide a partial solution, but the quality of the fish is usually inferior to those in the wild. Reducing the amount of fish that any one trawler or fishing boat is allowed to land is the most effective, but also the most unpopular measure. Countries in Europe like Spain rely heavily on fishing and are naturally against any step which restricts their catch, but if the depletion of fishing stocks continues there will be no fish left to fish! Take the disappearance of cod from the Great Banks off Newfoundland, which was once the richest cod fishing area in the Atlantic. After a dramatic fall in the cod population for some unknown reason, a ban was imposed which, it was hoped, would lead to a repopulation of the cod stocks. The cod did not return and many fishermen were put out of work. This is a scenario which we do not want to be repeated on a large scale.

Now if you look at this table on the screen, you can see …

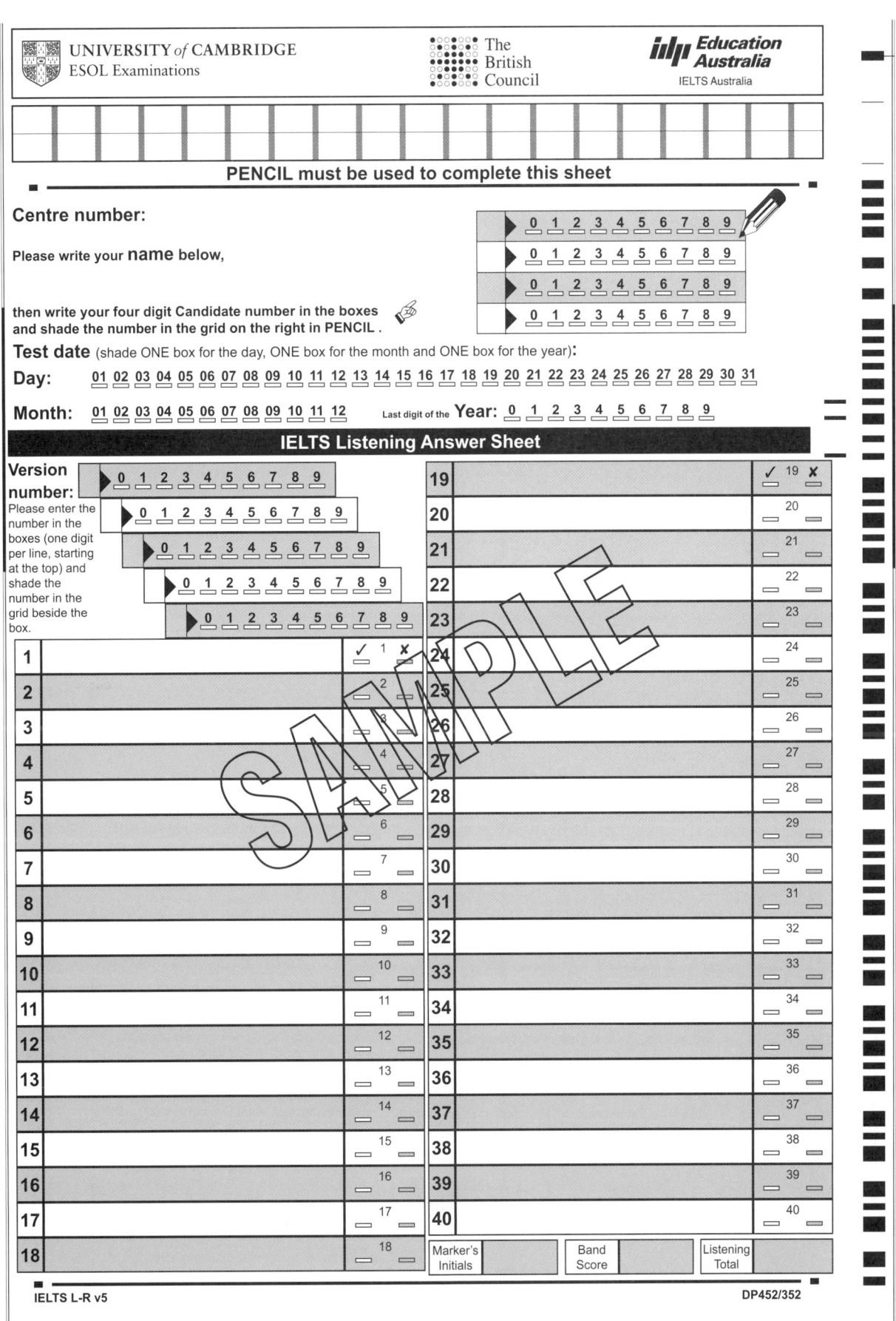

IELTS Reading Answer Sheet

Module taken (shade one box):　　Academic　⬜

　　　　　　　　　　　　　　　　　General Training　⬜

Version number:
Please enter the number in the boxes (one digit per line, starting at the top) and shade the number in the grid beside the box.

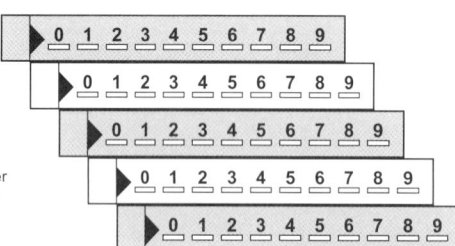

1		✓ 1 ✗	21		✓ 21 ✗
2		2	22		22
3		3	23		23
4		4	24		24
5		5	25		25
6		6	26		26
7		7	27		27
8		8	28		28
9		9	29		29
10		10	30		30
11		11	31		31
12		12	32		32
13		13	33		33
14		14	34		34
15		15	35		35
16		16	36		36
17		17	37		37
18		18	38		38
19		19	39		39
20		20	40		40

Marker's Initials		Band Score		Reading Total	

IELTS Results

After you have completed the IELTS test, you will receive a Test Report Form which details your score. For each module of the test (Listening, Reading, Writing and Speaking) you will receive a Band Score between 0 and 9. These individual module scores are then added together and averaged for an Overall Band Score reported as a whole band or a half band (e.g. 6.5). The table below gives a summary of the English of a candidate classified at each band level.

An IELTS Overall Band Score of 6.0 or 6.5 is usually required for entry to universities and colleges in Australia, New Zealand, Canada and the United Kingdom. However, some institutions may ask for a higher score.

BAND 9 – EXPERT USER

Has fully operational command of the language: appropriate, accurate and fluent with complete understanding.

BAND 8 – VERY GOOD USER

Has fully operational command of the language with only occasional unsystematic inaccuracies and inappropriacies. Misunderstandings may occur in unfamiliar situations. Handles complex detailed argumentation well.

BAND 7 – GOOD USER

Has operational command of the language, though with occasional inaccuracies, inappropriacies and misunderstandings in some situations. Generally handles complex language well and understands detailed reasoning.

BAND 6 – COMPETENT USER

Has generally effective command of the language despite some inaccuracies, inappropriacies and misunderstandings. Can use and understand fairly complex language, particularly in familiar situations.

BAND 5 – MODEST USER

Has partial command of the language, coping with overall meaning in most situations, though is likely to make many mistakes. Should be able to handle basic communication in own field.

BAND 4 – LIMITED USER

Basic competence is limited to familiar situations. Has frequent problems in understanding and expression. Is not able to use complex language.

BAND 3 – EXTREMELY LIMITED USER

Conveys and understands only general meaning in very familiar situations. Frequent breakdowns in communication occur.

BAND 2 – INTERMITTENT USER

No real communication is possible except for the most basic information using isolated words or short formulae in familiar situations and to meet immediate needs. Has great difficulty in understanding spoken and written English.

BAND 1 – NON USER

Essentially has no ability to use the language beyond possibly a few isolated words.

BAND 0 – DID NOT ATTEMPT THE TEST

No assessable information provided.

Reproduced by permission of University of Cambridge Local Examinations Syndicate.

CD ONE

1   Introduction

TEST ONE

2   Test instructions

Section 1

3   Instructions
4   Questions 1–5
5   Instructions
6   Questions 6–10
7   End of section instructions

Section 2

8   Instructions
9   Questions 11–13
10   Instructions
11   Questions 14–20
12   End of section instructions

Section 3

13   Instructions
14   Questions 21–23
15   Instructions
16   Questions 24–30
17   End of section instructions

Section 4

18   Instructions
19   Questions 31–33
20   Instructions
21   Questions 34–40
22   End of test instructions

TEST TWO

23   Test instructions

Section 1

24   Instructions
25   Questions 1–5
26   Instructions
27   Questions 6–10
28   End of section instructions

Section 2

29   Instructions
30   Questions 11–14
31   Instructions
32   Questions 15–20
33   End of section instructions

Section 3

34   Instructions
35   Questions 21–25
36   Instructions
37   Questions 26–30
38   End of section instructions

Section 4

39   Instructions
40   Questions 31–35
41   Instructions
42   Questions 36–40
43   End of test instructions

CD TWO

TEST THREE

1   Test instructions

Section 1

2   Instructions
3   Questions 1–5
4   Instructions
5   Questions 6–10
6   End of section instructions

Section 2

7   Instructions
8   Questions 11–13
9   Instructions
10   Questions 14–20
11   End of section instructions

Section 3

12   Instructions
13   Questions 21–24
14   Instructions
15   Questions 25–30
16   End of section instructions

Section 4

17   Instructions
18   Questions 31–35
19   Instructions
20   Questions 36–40
21   End of test instructions

TEST FOUR

22   Test instructions

Section 1

23   Instructions
24   Questions 1–6
25   Instructions
26   Questions 7–10
27   End of section instructions

Section 2

28   Instructions
29   Questions 11–14
30   Instructions
31   Questions 15–20
32   End of section instructions

Section 3

33   Instructions
34   Questions 21–24
35   Instructions
36   Questions 25–30
37   End of section instructions

Section 4

38   Instructions
39   Questions 31–36
40   Instructions
41   Questions 37–40
42   End of test instructions